Laurie Pippen's All Natural Colorants

for Cosmetic, Culinary, and Textile dyeing

Copyright 2015

Laurie Pippen

Laurie Pippen's All Natural Colorants
for Cosmetic, Culinary, and Textile Dyeing

Coloring with Plants & Plant Products

Colorants are everywhere. You can find dyes in your decor, cosmetics, food, and in nearly every fabric in the home from your socks to your furniture. Many of these dyes are made using chemical alternatives to the abundant selection of all natural colorants you can find cheaply and easily in your own backyard.

Whether you are hoping to make life more natural by creating your own, homemade colorants or hoping to replace one or two synthetic colorants with all natural plant dyes, you will find that coloring with natural choices is easy, fun, and yields amazing results.

A natural colorant is a colorant that comes from minerals, plants, or invertebrates. The most common natural colorants come from plant sources like bark, berries, flowers, leaves, and roots.

Potential dyeing options are everywhere and this book only illustrates the most traditionally used colorants and the methods I have employed to obtain my desired results. My favorite forms of natural dyes come from plant parts like berries, flowers, leaves, nuts, and roots. After reading this guide and gaining some skill with natural dyes, you should look around and experiment to see what new and creative natural colorants might be available in your own back yard.

Remember that natural colorants are not just for dyeing fabric.

You can use natural colorants to create homemade ink, paint, or even to dye Easter eggs. Some of our countries oldest documents were written with ink made from natural colorants.

You can also use natural colorants to make meals more healthy and appealing. Sometimes I like to use unusual colors to make mealtime fun for the whole family. Purple mashed potatoes or glowing orange rice is always a fun surprise.

You can even use plant products when you make personal care products like make up, soaps, and hair colorant. Many commercial cosmetics you purchase have their color roots in natural product dyes and with a little knowledge and a bit of practice, you can become a master at making pleasing looking and smelling products for your family that actually have benefits to go with their attractiveness.

Nearly anything you work with that needs color is a potential choice for natural plant dyes! Natural colorants come in every shade you might want. You can even blend or tone the colors up and down to achieve the exact result you need for your project.

The first step to dyeing using natural colorants is to select and process the plant parts you will use to create your dye. Reviewing the plant colorant options is important to help you learn what plants will yield the results you want and to understand which plant colorants might prove beneficial in ways beyond aesthetics.

Before using a natural colorant in food or cosmetic products, you should review the potential supplemental effects of the colorant. Plant products are wonderful choices for living a more natural life, but many plant products contain compounds that have an effect on the body. It is important for anyone experimenting with natural products to gain a comprehensive knowledge of the plants they use.

Selecting & Using Plant Parts

One of the most frequently asked questions about plant colorants is when to harvest plant parts to obtain the best color.

The best color usually comes from fresh plants harvested at their peak blooming time. Certain plants may yield better color at other times during their growing cycle, but when you are just starting with natural colorants, it is best to select plants at their peak bloom time.

The easiest plant parts to use for starter colorants are flowers and fruits. Flowers and fruits often color similar to their appearance and yield up the colorants more easily, making them a fun starting point for natural dyeing.

You should remember that some plants might actually yield a different color depending on the time of day they are harvested, how warm, wet, or windy the season has been, or for another reason entirely. Do not become discouraged if the first batch of colorants you create does not yield exactly the tone that you expect. Half of the fun of making homemade colorants is the joy of discovery. That new, accidentally created color might just become your favorite.

As you become more familiar with the processes of making natural colorants, you will want to explore other plant parts like barks, leaves, roots, even nuts. You should get to know as many plants as possible. Some plants may give you a preferred color only after they have bloomed and lost their luster. Others may give you the color you want when the buds first appear. The more time you spend observing nature, the more versatile your coloring options will become.

In general, you should gather flowers while they are in full bloom and berries & nuts when they are ripe.

You will need to clean the plant parts to remove any residue, dirt, or other matter before extracting the colorants.

You will cut the plant parts you intend to use as a coloring agent into smaller parts to help expose as many of the cells as possible to the bath.

Exposing many cells helps to decrease the time you will need to extract the colorants and encourages the plant to yield up its color more easily.

You will need to crush some harder plant parts to obtain the best color results.

Once you have selected the dye plants you wish to use, you will need to extract the colorant.

The most common way to extract plant colorant is through a water bath. In general, the more plant material you use compared to water, the deeper the colorant will be in the final product. Other bath bases exist, and will be defined as you move through the learning process, but water is a wonderful starting point for creating natural colorants.

In the beginning, you will want to use fresh plants for colorants if possible. As you gain in knowledge and skill, you will gain an understanding of which plants you can harvest, dry, and store for later use without altering the color potency.

You can purchase pre-dried materials, but the most satisfying projects are often those you create yourself from beginning to end. As such, you should gain a fundamental understanding of plant drying processes. There are many ways to dry plant parts. Each of them has benefits and drawbacks. The three basic methods that are most often used for drying plants are air-drying, speed drying, and hang drying.

Air Drying

Air-drying is exactly how it sounds. You will expose the parts of the plant to the air to allow the moisture to evaporate. A few plants do well when air and sun are combined during the process but most should be kept out of direct sunlight since it can evaporate or damage the beneficial compounds you are trying to obtain.

Air-drying is the slowest method of drying plant products but it often allows the plant parts to retain more beneficial compounds.

Before starting the air-drying process, you should decide where you are going to dry the plants. If the weather is just right, you may be able to dry the plants outside away from direct sunlight and the elements. More often, you will want to select an area inside the home where the plant will not be disturbed during drying.

The biggest consideration is that the area you select must be very dry. Plants will not dry properly in a space with high humidity.

The second consideration is that the area should not get extreme air movement from nature, fans, door closures, people, or another source. As the plant parts dry, they will become light. A good breeze will scatter the plants and ruin the project.

You should also consider the container you will use to dry your plants. There are many different types of air-drying racks available for purchase. Many of these allow you to stack the plants for drying. These are very convenient and some are even pretty. Depending on the amount of air-drying you will do, purchasing drying racks can become costly. If you want to keep costs low or will only be drying plants occasionally, you can make your own drying bins. A simple rack can be made by layering a clean cotton towel or waxed paper inside a shallow cookie sheet or even a cardboard box. Whatever bins you choose must not be able to absorb the compounds from your plant, must not contaminate the plant, must allow you to dry the plant parts in one layer not a pile, and must be durable enough to withstand the turning or agitation of the plant parts.

Once you have selected the container for your drying processes, you will need to finish preparing the plant parts.

The cleaned, dried herbs will need to be broken down into smaller pieces. It is often beneficial to break the plants into smaller pieces prior to drying. This not only saves you time later, it speeds the drying process since smaller parts give more air exposure and thus a faster drying process. You can pull the leaves, flowers, and stems apart with your hands or use a pair of clean shears to achieve the right size.

Place the plant pieces into the prepared container in one thin layer. This helps ensure more plant parts are exposed to the air. The more parts exposed to the air, the faster the plant materials will dry. The faster the plant materials dry, the less likely they are to develop mold growth.

Different plants will dry at different rates. You will want to agitate or turn your plant parts at least one time each day. The more moisture you have in the air or in the plant, the more frequently you will want to turn the mixture. The goal with agitating the plant parts is to ensure that everything dries evenly and quickly.

It is important that the plants dry as quickly as possible. If you enter a very humid period during the drying process, you may need to place the drying containers in the oven to help prevent excess moisture build up and mold growth.

Oven Assisted Plant Drying
You can speed dry the plant parts in the oven. This is not one of my favorite methods because you run the risk of cooking the plant parts instead of simply drying them. There are times when oven drying may be the only logical solution like when a high humidity day hits in the middle of the drying process. It may be a better choice to risk cooking the herbs rather than risk losing the entire batch to mold.

If you choose to use the oven assist drying method, you need to make certain your oven is clean and free of chemicals. Any chemicals in the oven may pollute your plant products.

You should turn the oven on to its lowest setting and leave the door open to its first 'notch' or about 4 inches. This helps to allow air into the drying process and to keep the oven from becoming too warm.

You will need to array your plant parts as thinly as possible on the drying mat. A perforated oven-safe tray works best for oven assist drying. If you do not have an oven-safe tray, you can layer clean cotton or paper towels across the oven racks. Place the plant products onto the chosen holder.

The herbs will dry very quickly in the oven so you should check them every couple of minutes to ensure they do not over dry or 'cook'. The amount of time you will need to dry the plants will depend on the type of plant product you are using, the amount of moisture remaining in the plants, the humidity in the air, and other factors.

When you check the plants you will want to agitate them like you would during air-drying. This will help the plant parts to dry more evenly. If you are using a soft cloth and can safely pick up the drying tray, just bouncing the plant parts a few times may be a sufficient method of agitation. If you are using a solid rack, turn the herbs every few minutes.

Speed Drying Herbs

Food dehydrators have completely changed the way some people dry their herbs. A dehydrator follows the same basic concept as air-drying it just does the job much more quickly. The dehydrator forces warm, dry air around the plant parts. This helps to remove the moisture from the plants more quickly and actually makes a more pleasing final product for some plant parts like oily fruit rinds, wood bark, and nuts.

The dehydrator must have a fan and allow you to set the heat setting extremely low or else you will cook your plants just as you would in an overheated oven. If the dehydrator you are using has a recommendation in the manual for drying herbs, you should start with those instructions and then adapt the settings to suit your particular needs. If there are no recommendations, start the process with the temperature on the lowest setting, usually around 90°, and gradually increase the temperature if you feel the plants are drying too slowly.

You will spread the plant parts onto the dehydrator trays in a single layer. You should make your layer loose so there is plenty of room for airflow to reach all sides of the plants.

The dehydrator will complete the drying process much more quickly than air-drying. You should check the plants every 15 – 20 minutes. At each check, you may want to rotate the trays. The plant parts closest to the heat source will dry more quickly and rotating the trays helps to distribute the airflow & heat. You should remove the plant parts as they become dry enough for use.

Hang Drying Plants

Hang Drying is an easy way to dry plants that works well if you have plenty of space and a controlled room where you can hang the plants. Hang drying also helps to produce a stronger final product when you are going to be using only the flowers & leaves.

You will want to be certain there are no contaminants in the room for the plants to absorb during drying and that the air is very low in humidity. I use hang drying in the winter months since heating the house often serves a dual purpose of removing humidity from the air. Drying herbs in a closed house also helps to brighten and freshen the house naturally.

When you harvest for hang drying, you will leave longer stems on the plants. The stems will be used for the hanging. Cut each plant as close to the same length as you can.

Gather the ends of the stems together. You can use a pasta measure to judge how much you have gathered clumping about 1 serving worth per hanging group. If you make the hanging group too large, it will take longer to dry and you risk ruining the batch if the air cannot reach the middle plants.

Tie the gathered stems into a bouquet about 2 inches from the ends using natural string or jute. You will want to tie the stems tightly enough that they do not fall out of the clump but not so tightly that you break the stem. Leave an extra length of string to hook the clump to your hanger.

The stems will shrink as they dry so you may want to check the bundle occasionally to ensure that the tie has not loosened so much that you are losing stems.

Hang the herbs upside down with the cut stems facing toward the ceiling. This helps the compounds in the plant travel toward the leaves & flowers strengthening the final product.

Hang drying makes seed capture easy if you plan to propagate a new batch of plants. Place a bin, paper bag, or cardboard box underneath the hanging plant. The bin will capture any plant parts or seeds that fall off when the plant becomes dry enough to release them.

The amount of time necessary for hang drying will depend on the temperature of the area, humidity in the air, moisture in the plant, density of the plant, and other factors. You should check the plants regularly to see if they are ready for storage.

Storing the Dried Product
Each plant product will dry at a different rate and you should check often to see if any of the matter is ready for use or storage. You will become adept at judging the progress of the drying by sight. You should be able to see & feel a gradual reduction in the moisture of the plant parts.

Select a leaf or flower and hold it between your thumb and forefinger. Gently rub your fingers back and forth. The leaf or flower will break into tiny pieces without much effort. It should not powder. If the plant parts powder as soon as you touch them, they are too dry. Over-drying the plant parts diminishes the power of the active compounds.

At times, you will be drying flower buds or berries. These will appear different when dry from a leaf or flower petal. Select a berry or flower bud and look at it closely. It should look and feel like a hardened raisin. When it feels like a hardened raisin, it is ready for storage or use.

Stems and twigs dry differently than other plant parts. Select a stem or twig that appears to be dry and try to snap it into smaller pieces. Fully dried stems & twigs will snap easily much like a piece of uncooked spaghetti.

Seeds and nuts can be dried and broken to check their readiness for storage. Select a nut or seed and place it on a hard surface like a cutting board and then attempt to crush it with a kitchen mallet, the bottom of a ceramic cup, or the side of your shears. Nuts & seeds should break into a powder that does not clump easily. If the powder is still clumping, there are likely too many oils in the nut or seed and you should allow them to dry further before storage. If the powder is fine and easily sifted, the seeds or nuts are ready to be ground into flour for storage or use or stored whole until you are ready for them.

If you are still not certain your plant parts are ready for storage, you can select a small amount of the plant and place it in a clean, dry glass jar. Seal the lid tightly and place the jar in a warm, sunny location. If moisture condenses inside the jar over the first few hours, the plant is not ready for storage. If no moisture appears, the plant part is dry enough for storage.

You should store your newly dried plant product in a way that will not allow moisture or contaminants to permeate back into the dried goods. Some people use special stainless steel storage cans while others make "bags" from waxed paper. Porcelain, ceramic, and glass are other common choices. You should choose whatever storage method works best in your household. You do need to select a storage container that blocks moisture, light, and chemical contaminants.

Most correctly dried pant parts will retain many of their beneficial compounds for 1 year after the harvesting and storage date.

Freezing Plants

Sometimes, plant parts need to be harvested at a time that is not conducive to drying or the parts just do not dry properly. When this happens, another option is to freeze the plants.

Some people make freezing their primary method of storage for all of their harvests. If you do not have a dry room, live in a moist climate, or are unable to air dry the plant parts for another reason, freezing may be an alternative for you. You should remember that freezing is not technically a drying method and a great deal of the moisture will remain in the plant parts making any supplement made from freeze-dried plants weaker than their traditionally dried counterparts do.

Freezing is actually a simpler method of storing. You will harvest and clean the plant parts the same way that you do in any storage process. After the excess water has been removed, strip the leaves, petals, and any other plant parts you plan to save. Place the usable pieces in the freezer storage container you have selected. The faster you freeze the parts the better, so a deep freezer or the quick freeze shelf in some side-by-side freezers is a good choice. The plant parts should be good for use for 3-4 months.

Using Dried Plant Parts

When you are ready to use the dried plant parts as a direct coloring agent for projects like the creation of cosmetics, culinary dishes, or other recipe based projects, you may want to turn your dried parts into a powder colorant.

If you picture the colorant like you would a spice you will have an idea of how the powdered product should appear. Turmeric is an example of a powdered plant product that is frequently used as a culinary colorant.

You can powder most plant parts using a food processor, blender, or mortar and pestle.

The powder can be blended with other ingredients to alter the tone. When you have blended the powders to the color you desire, you can add it to the liquid base necessary for your project to activate the colorants. The color achieved with a powdered product will not be as pure or as long lasting as those achieved with larger plant parts but when you are using them in cosmetic or culinary projects, the projects are shorter lasting making this a non-issue.

Traditional Dye Bath

The colorants that are in the plant can be extracted using the water bath method whether you are using fresh, frozen, or dried plant parts.

When dyeing using a water bath, you will simply adjust the expected color, strength of the dye bath, and amount of liquid needed to extract the colorants based on the type of plant product you are using.

A dried plant will require more water and will yield a lighter tone than a fresh plant.

A frozen plant may contain more liquid depending on the way it was stored. You should adjust the amount of water you use in your dye bath to compensate for the excess moisture in a frozen plant.

You should cut, crush, or bruise fresh plant parts as you would if you were going to dry them. This helps to ensure that as many plant parts contact the water as possible making the color extraction stronger.

After you have selected and prepared your plant parts, you will make a dye bath using the plant products and water.

The pot you use for the dye bath should be made of glass or enamel. A pot made of iron, aluminum, steel, or copper will alter the dye color and change the final product.

You can make your dye bath in one pot and then move the colorant before dyeing your fabric or you can use the same pot throughout the process. If you are going to prepare the dye bath and color fabric or other matter in the same pot, you will need one that is large enough for the materials you are coloring to move freely. If the materials are not able to spread out in the pan, the dye will not set evenly.

The water you use for extraction and dyeing should be soft water. Most tap water is too hard to achieve the results you want from the dye bath. You can obtain spring water, collect rainwater, purchase or make filtered water, or add a softener to the tap water. Some plant materials, like madder will require harder water but in general, soft water is a better selection.

Traditionally 1 part plant material to 1 part water works well for extraction. This will yield a medium dye product. Higher amounts of plant material will yield a more intense final color. Less plant material will give a softer color.

The type of product to be dyed, plant being used, and desired colorant will determine how much plant matter you need. A good rule is that you should use 1 pound of plant matter to 1 pound of product to be dyed.

Increasing or decreasing the ratio or allowing the fabric to soak for a longer period during the dyeing stage will alter the color.

Any time you change from 1 part plant to 1 part water or change the soak time, keep notes on what you did to enable you to duplicate the results in the future. Remember, natural colorants can yield nearly any shade you desire, but in order to duplicate the results in the future, you should have written notes for reference.

Place the plant products and water into your pot. Bring the mixture to a boil. The boiling time will depend on the toughness of the materials you are using as well as the colorant. Some plant materials yield color more easily than other materials.

Tougher plant products may boil for an hour or more depending on the depth of color you want from your dye bath. Some plant products or even specific colors are more delicate than others are. An example would be red and yellow colorants. Using too much heat with reds and yellows can sometimes damage the pigments. When dyeing, it is always better to use caution. Begin by bringing the mixture to a boil and immediately removing it from the heat. Check the tone of the bath. The actual tone will continue to bleed into the water over the coming hours so you are not looking at the tone at the moment, what you are looking for is a release of any colorant. If the plants appear to be releasing the colorant, you can move on to the next step. If the water has very little color bleed, return it to the heat. Again, make notes to remind you how you achieved your desired results so you can duplicate them in the future.

When the boiling process is complete, turn off the heat and allow the mixture to steep for an average of 6-12 hours though some plant materials can steep for up to 48 hours. Some plant material will release color very quickly while other materials will take longer. You can control the color tone by checking the dye bath frequently so you can move onto the next step when the bath reaches the desired shade.

When you have achieved the color you want for your dye bath, strain the plant material from the liquid.

The liquid that remains will be your dye bath.

Using the Dye Bath

You can add the dye bath directly to culinary recipes, cosmetics, or paint products. When adding the dye bath results to a recipe, cosmetic, or craftwork product, replace the liquid called for in the recipe with the dye bath liquid. For example if the recipe calls for:

½ cup water   =   ½ cup dye bath
1 teaspoon juice =   1 teaspoon dye bath

The dye bath will most frequently be used to color fabric. Fabric requires a few extra steps to make the dye product colorfast against washing, weathering, and other usage.

Preparing the Fabric

You will want to prepare your fabric or materials for the dye bath.

Weigh the material you will be using in the dye process so you can ensure that you have enough dye to color the entire batch of fabric at the same time. This will help prevent color variation between batches and make your finished product nicer. Remember, the standard is 1 pound of fabric to 1 cup of dried plant parts extracted in 1 cup of fluid.

You should pre-rinse the fabric by hand or in the washer.

Most materials will need to be washed using a detergent to remove any residue that might interfere with the dye absorption.

You can place the fabric in the washer or hot water to a rinse bath made with 1-teaspoon washing soda, detergent, or another cleaner per pound of fabric.

If you are working with materials like raw wool, you will need to scour the fabric to remove the oils. I like to cook my wool fabrics, but you can remove the oils in any way that works well for you. I use 4 gallons of water to 1 tablespoon of detergent for each pound of wool I am scouring.

Simmer the scouring solution containing your fabric for 30-45 minutes. Allow the liquid to cool and then rinse the residue from the fabric.

If your fabric is already free of residue, you will still need to wet the fabric before you add it to the dye bath. The wetting helps the fabric to absorb the colorant.

Selecting a Mordant

Some dye products will color well when used alone. Some plants act as a self-mordant meaning that they contain properties that help to fix the color and do not require the use of a separate mordant. These are often termed direct dye or substantive dyes. Many plant based dye products do need a mordant.

A mordant is a chemical that prepares the fabric for dyeing, helps the fibers absorb the colorant, and fixes the dye to the fabric to make the color permanent. A mordant may also change the color of a dye, giving the dyer the opportunity to obtain a wide-range of color options from the same plant.

Some projects lend themselves to temporary colorants. You may prefer temporary colorants when making children's craft items, cosmetics, or other temporary projects. Most dye projects require longevity of the color. You will use a mordant as a fixative to ensure the colors do not fade over time.

A mordant helps to set the colorant into the fabric. The mordant you select will also change the color of the finished dye product. You will want to experiment with a variety of combinations to see what colors they yield and how each color can benefit your finished product.

There are three commonly used methods of using a mordant for dyeing.

Pre-Mordanting means you will rinse or soak the fabric to be dyed with the mordant before adding the fabric to the dye bath. Alum is the most commonly used pre-mordant, but other mordant options are occasionally used in a pre-mordant bath.

Meta-Mordanting means you will add the selected mordant to the dye bath and blend it into the liquid before adding the fabric. Applying the mordant at the same time you apply the colorant is faster and some people always select this method. Meta-Mordanting can sometimes cause uneven results. You should dissolve the mordant in a bit of water before adding it to the dye bath to help ensure it blends more evenly.

Post-Mordanting means you will treat the fabric with the mordant bath or rinse after the coloring has been completed. Post-Mordanting is most frequently used when the color tone of a particular plant needs to be changed. For example, if a colorant is too deep, alum will sometimes help to ease the tone when it is applied as a post-mordant. If the color is bland or not as appealing as you expected, using a post-mordant like copper can help to make the color more appealing by giving a green tone to the fabric.

The timing of the application of the mordant will affect the color results. The type of mordant you select will also affect the shade and the color fastness of the finished results.

The amount of time each fiber is left in the mordant will also affect the color and colorfastness of the results. The soak time will vary depending numerous factors including the tone desired, the strength of the fabric, the potential use of the fabric, and the colorfastness needed from the fabric.

In general, you will simmer cotton, course fibers, and silk in the mordant for up to 1 hour followed by up to 24 hours of soak time. You will simmer wool in the mordant for 1 to 2 hours, allow the mixture to cool, and then rinse the fabric immediately. Some fabrics or projects will not bear up to simmering. When working with a fabric that cannot have a direct application of heat, you will heat the mordant water and then remove it from the heat source before adding the fabric.

The mordant will soak into the fiber and open it to accept the dye. If you have pre-mordanted the fiber, you will rinse it before adding it to the dye bath. This does not remove the mordant. It does remove any remaining residue from the mordant bath. If you are meta-mordanting the mordant and the dye bath will both be rinsed at the end of the process.

There are many mordants available for use as a fixative. The selection of the mordant depends on many factors including your personal preference, the dye plant, and the type of fabric being colored.

Some plants work best with one type of mordant or another. Some mordants will help to alter, brighten, or darken the color provided by a particular plant. Different fabrics may react better with one type of mordant over a different one.   The entries in the common mordant and modifier section of this book will help you to determine the best mordants for your desired results, plant dye, and fabric.

In addition to the mordant, you may choose to use anther additive known as a modifier. A modifier is a chemical that helps to assist dyeing, aids the mordant in fixing the color, and changes the dye bath to a more acid or alkali condition. A modifier will change the effect of the dye product on the fiber but is not strong enough to work by itself.

The plant guide chapter illustrates some of the results you can expect with a specific mordant, modifier, & plant blend. This does not mean that the combination is the only way you can use the particular plant colorant. This does mean the combination noted is the combination I used to achieve the results I desired. Other combinations will give you different results. You can experiment with a variety of mordant and colorant blends to achieve new colors that are truly your own.

The one caution to experimentation is that you should never use too much mordant. Less mordant will create a paler final product. Using the quantity of mordant recommended here or by the mordant supplier yields the noted color tone. Adding more mordant to the mixture will not necessarily deepen the final product beyond the expected results. Adding more mordant than the maximum recommendation is most likely going to result in damaged fibers instead of a better color tone.

Common Mordents & Modifiers

Acid dyes are soluble in water and used to increase the effectiveness of dyes on protein fibers like silk & wool.

Acid dyes are also frequently used when coloring food.

Acetic Acid
Description:
Acetic Acid is most often used in the form of Vinegar. Vinegar is a colorless liquid modifier consisting of acetic acid and water. It has been used for thousands of years as a dye solvent & fixative. Other forms of acetic acid are used in dyeing to achieve different results of as a personal preference.

Common Uses:
Acetic Acid is traditionally used to even out dye color especially in protein fibers.

Acetic Acid is used as an aid in coloring silk and wool fabrics.

Acetic Acid tends to give a reddish undertone to the dye bath especially when using blue, brown, or purple colorants.

Acetic Acid is used to help neutralize an alkaline dye bath.

Acetic Acid is commonly used as a component in the creation of culinary colorants.

Best Fabric:
Protein Fibers, Silk, Wool

Amounts:
Acetic Acid is used as an alkaline neutralizer at an approximate rate of ¼-cup acetic acid to 1-pound fiber and 3 gallons of liquid.

Acetic Acid is added as a pre-dye modifier at a rate of 2 teaspoons acetic acid to 3 gallons mordant bath and as a post-dye modifier at a rate of 2-

teaspoon acetic acid to 3 gallons mordant bath per pound of fabric allowed to soak for approximately 1 hour.

Acetic Acid, Vinegar
Description:
Vinegar is a distilled liquid commonly used as a culinary ingredient and as a dye solvent or modifier. Any vinegar can be used but white vinegar is the most commonly selected since it does not transfer color of its own to the fibers.

Common Uses:
Vinegar is used to even out the dye color.

Vinegar helps fibers to absorb mordants and colorants more efficiently.

Vinegar neutralizes harsh mordants.

Vinegar is used to give a reddish tone to blue & purple colorants.

Best Fabric:
Silk, Wool

Amounts:
Vinegar is used at every stage of the dye process. A good starting pre-mordant mixture is 3 tablespoons of vinegar to 1 gallon of water. If it is acting as a meta-mordant additive, you will use 1-tablespoon of vinegar to 1-pound of fabric added before simmering the mixture. If it is being used as a post-mordant rinse agent, you will add 3-tablespoons vinegar to 1-pound of fabric.

Vinegar is frequently used for culinary colorants as it is edible, helps to deepen the tone of the colorants, and provides lasting results. Most Easter egg kits use chemical dye pellets modified with vinegar to give lasting, deep color to the eggs.

Alum
Description:

Alum is a chemical compound that helps to purify water and causes a dye bath to become more gel-like helping the colorant adhere better to the project. Alum is considered an acid mordant

Common Uses:
Alum is used as a fixative giving color fastness to a variety of fabric types.

Alum is used to brighten the color tone of a dye bath.

Best Fabric:
Any

Amounts:
A good starting mix is 3 tablespoons of alum to 1 pound of fabric.

Alum should never exceed ¼ of the final weight of the fabric. Lower amounts of alum will yield a lighter finished tone.

Overuse:
Alum will destroy cellulose fibers if left on the fabric for an extended time.

Overuse of Alum will cause most fibers to become sticky.

Blends:
Alum is sometimes mixed with cream of tarter to give a smoother dye result. A standard blend is 1 part alum to 1 part cream of tarter.

Aluminum Acetate
Description:
Aluminum Acetate is a water-soluble powder used as an acid based mordant especially when dyeing with red colorants.

Common Uses:
Aluminum Acetate is commonly used to dye cotton fiber.

Aluminum Acetate is sometimes hyper-heated to add a waterproofing element to fabric.

Best Fabric:
Cotton - Waterproofing

Amounts:
A good starting mix is 4 tablespoons of Aluminum Acetate to 1 pound of fabric.

Aluminum Acetate should never exceed a ratio of 1:4 of the final weight of the fabric. Lower amounts of aluminum acetate will yield a lighter finished tone but too high of a ratio may damage the fabric.

Aluminum Ammonium Sulfate
Description:
Aluminum Ammonium Sulfate is also sometimes called Alum. It is an acid mordant derived from salt mines or plant salts. Aluminum Ammonium Sulfate is often used when a more natural product is desirable or for dyeing cellulose fibers.

Common Uses:
Aluminum Ammonium Sulfate is commonly used to dye cellulose based fabrics.

Aluminum Ammonium Sulfate is used as a mordant alternative when a more natural product is desirable.

Best Fabric:
Cellulose, Cotton

Amounts:
A good starting mix is 2 tablespoons of Aluminum Ammonium Sulfate to 1 pound of fabric.

Aluminum Ammonium Sulfate should never exceed ¼ of the final weight of the fabric. Lower amounts of Aluminum Ammonium Sulfate will yield a lighter finished tone.

Overuse:

Aluminum Ammonium Sulfate should only be used in non-heat mordanting as heating can cause chemical changes that may be toxic.

Ammonium Acetate
Description:
Ammonium Acetate is a colorless acid modifier commonly used to remove excess coloration and to enhance red dye products.

Common Uses:
Ammonium Acetate is used as a dye pot additive or post-dye rinse to remove excess coloration.

Ammonium Acetate is used as an enhancer in some dye baths most commonly when using red tones.

Best Fabric:
Silk

Amounts:
Add small amounts of Ammonium Acetate to a dye bath or rinse beginning with 1/8 teaspoon per pound of fabric.

Ammonium Sulfate
Description:
Ammonium Sulfate is an acid modifier used to increase the acidity of a dye bath.

Common Uses:
Ammonium Sulfate is added to a dye bath to level the colorant.

Ammonium Sulfate increases the acidity of a dye bath as heat is applied to the colorant.

Best Fabric:
Cotton

Amounts:

A good starting mix is 3 tablespoons of Ammonium Sulfate to 1 pound of fabric.

Oxalic Acid
Description:
Oxalic Acid is an odorless powder derived from some plants like wood sorrels. It is primarily used as an acid modifier in dyeing.

Common Uses:
Oxalic Acid acts to help increase the fixative effect of alum and copper.

Oxalic Acid helps to reduce the yellow tones of green colorants.

Best Fabric:
Silk, Wool

Amounts:
Oxalic Acid is traditionally used as a pre-mordant rinse at a rate of 1 tablespoon Oxalic Acid per pound of fabric simmered for 1 hour and allowed to steep for up to 1 month.

Citric Acid
Description:
Citric Acid is used as an acid modifier in dye baths and is most frequently added as either lime or lemon juice.

Common Uses:
Citric Acid is added to the dye bath to adjust the pH allowing colors to fix more readily.

Citric Acid enables fibers to absorb most mordant and colorants more efficiently.

Citric Acid is used to brighten colors.

Citric Acid helps to give a reddish tone to blue and purple colorants.

Citric Acid is used as a post dye rinse agent to help remove excess color.

Best Fabric:
Silk, Wool

Amounts:
Citric Acid is used sparingly in the dye bath or as a post-colorant rinse agent starting at a rate of 1 teaspoon of juice or 1/8 teaspoon of powder.

Lime
Description:
Lime can be either slaked or unslaked and has been used as an alkali modifier in dye baths since ancient times for its ability to neutralize acids without creating an alkaline solution.

Common Uses:
Lime is added to a dye bath to enhance most colorants.

Lime is used to alter the colorant yield from some wood dyes.

Best Fabric:
Cellulose Fibers

Baking Soda
Description:
Baking Soda is a common household item consisting of baking powder and tartaric acid. Baking Soda is used as an alkali modifier in the dye bath.

Common Uses:
Baking Soda is used to soften the water used in dyeing.

Baking Soda brightens the color tone of a dye bath.

Baking Soda alters the acidity of a dye bath.

Add baking soda to the dye bath before simmering to enhance blue, green, purple, and red tones.

Use baking soda as a post dye rinse to enhance blue, burgundy, and purple tones.

Best Fabric:
Cellulose Fibers

Amounts:
Baking soda is traditionally added as a simmering component at a rate of 2 teaspoons per pound of fabric.

Baking Soda is used as a final rinse at a rate of 4 teaspoons to pound of fabric.

Calcium Carbonate, Chalk
Description:
Calcium Carbonate is a neutral modifier that is used in dye baths to neutralize acids without increasing alkaline.

Common Uses:
Calcium Carbonate is used in certain dye baths to make water harder.

Calcium Carbonate is used to lower the acidity of a dye bath.

Calcium Carbonate is used to enhance the color achieved when using certain plants, like madder, that produce better in hard water.

Calcium Carbonate is used to aid in enhancing colors and as a fixative for wood-based dyes.

Best Fabric:
Cellulose Fiber

Amounts:
Add small amounts of Calcium Carbonate to a dye bath or post bath rinse beginning with 1/8 teaspoon per pound of fabric.

Chrome, Chromium
Description:
Chrome is used as a pre-mordant and acts as a brightener for green, reds, and yellows.

Common Uses:
Chromium mordant is traditionally applied to the fabric before the dye.

Chrome is usually used to brighten the warmer tones of the dye bath.

Chrome enhances green, red, and yellow colorants brightening and warming the overall effect.

The colors achieved with a chrome mordant will be more permanent, staying color fast to washing, weathering, and light exposure.

Best Fabric:
Cellulose Fibers, Wool, Wool Blends

Amounts:
A good starting mixture is 1 tablespoon of chrome to pound of fabric.

Overuse:
Chrome tends to be very caustic and care should be taken to protect the skin during use. The dyer should take care to keep the air flowing during use to minimize the respiration of fumes. Any dye bath containing Chrome remaining after the project is complete should be disposed of as hazardous waste.

Blends:
Chrome is often blended with cream of tarter at a rate of 1 part chrome to 1 part cream of tarter.

Copper, Copper Sulfate
Description:

Copper Sulfate is an odorless mordant used to give good color fastness to fabric.

Common Uses:
Copper is traditionally used as a mordant to help increase the green tones of a colorant and to darken the color result of a dye bath.

Copper is sometimes used alone as a dye product to give a pale green tone to fabric.

Copper Sulfate can also be used a modifier applied after the colorant to bring out any green tone in the dye or alter the color to your personal taste.

Best Fabric:
Cellulose Fibers, Silk, Wool

Amounts:
Copper can be applied to the fabric as a pre-mordant, meta-mordant, or post mordant at a rate of 1 teaspoon of copper per pound of fabric.

Blends:
2 parts vinegar to 1 part copper is sometimes used to improve the absorption of copper.

2 parts salt to 1 part copper is used to make copper more colorfast.

Cream of Tarter
Description:
Cream of Tarter is a common household ingredient used as an alkaline modifier in dye baths. Cream of Tarter is used to help limit damage to the fibers being dyed. It is most often used for tin and alum mordant baths. Cream of Tarter also helps to brighten and soften the fabric.

Common Uses:
Cream of Tarter is used to soften fibers and provide some protection when a harsh mordant is used in a dye bath.

Cream of Tarter helps enhance the fixative qualities of a mordant and prevent fading from washings.

Cream of Tarter helps brighten colors of a dye bath.

Best Fabric:
Silk, Wool

Cream of Tarter may block absorption of colorants in cellulose fibers.

Amounts:
Cream of Tarter is used as a meta-mordant but should be added only after any heating has been completed.

Cream of Tarter is used at a starting rate of 2 tablespoons per pound of fabric.

Ferrous Sulfate, Iron
Description:
Iron is a powder that turns brown when exposed to air. It is derived mainly from clay, rocks, and sand.

Common Uses:
Iron is used to darken and dull the tone of a colorant. It will add a gray undertone to the final product when used in the dye bath or as an after dye modifier.

Iron will help to tone yellow or gold dye baths a soft green.

Iron will help to tone red colorants into a burgundy.

Iron also adds a grey tone to almost any tannin based dye product.

Best Fabric:
Cotton, Linen, Silk, Wool

Amounts:
A good starting mixture is 1 teaspoon of iron per pound of fabric.

Many dyers add iron to the dye bath at the end of the dyeing process and extend the simmering time by 20-30 minutes to allow the iron to take.

Overuse:
Overuse of iron mordant will cause the fabric to become fragile.

Blends:
Iron is often blended with Cream of Tarter at a rate of 1 part iron to 2 parts Cream of Tarter.

Alcohol, Ethyl Alcohol, Methyl Alcohol
Description:
Alcohol is a colorless liquid used to help oxidize dye products like bark, wood, and other tough textiles helping to extract the color. Ethyl & Methyl alcohol are traditionally used for textile dyeing and consumables like grain & vodka are used as a component in culinary colorant creation.

Common Uses:
Alcohol is used to make minor modifications to the final color of a fabric when it is over-dyed or the tone is off from the desired color.

Alcohol is used to oxidize wood dye products.

Best Fabric:
Any

Amounts:
Alcohol is added when making a dye bath from wood-based colorants. The wood should be ground or powdered and added at a rate of 3 tablespoons wood powder to 1cup of alcohol. Blend the ingredients into dough. Cover and allow the mixture to oxidize 4 to 24 hours. Agitate the mixture every hour during the oxidization process. Use the resulting product in the desired dye bath.

Potash
Description:

Potash is a white powder substance commonly used in manufacturing of soap products. It is a strong alkali modifier commonly used with wood-based colorants.

Common Uses:
Potash is commonly used with wood-based dye baths like logwood to help them yield a firmer color. When used with logwood, potash yields true black.

Best Fabric:
Cellulose

Amounts:
Potash is used sparingly in the dye bath at a starting rate of 1/8 teaspoon powder per pound of fabric.

Salt, Sodium Sulfate
Description:
Salt is a natural substance extracted from seawater and commonly used as a culinary seasoning. Salt is also used as a modifier or extender in dye processes.

Common Uses:
Salt is commonly used as a post dye bath rinse to fix the color while speeding up the drying process.

Salt is added to an acid dye bath to help the colorant take more evenly.

Salt is used to enhance red or blue colorants.

Salt will increase the yellow tones of a green dye bath.

Salt is most frequently used for berry dyes but can be used to smooth a variety of dye bath solutions.

Best Fabric:
Any

Amounts:

Salt is generally used at a starting rate of ½ cup to 1-gallon fluid or 1-gallon rinse agent.

Salt is most frequently used for berry dyes at a rate of ¼-cup salt to 4 cups water +/-.

Blends:

Vinegar is sometimes added at a rate of 2 tablespoons per gallon of salt water to create stronger, bolder colors.

Smoke
Description:

Smoke from open fires has been used as both a modifier and fixative in dyeing.

Common Uses:

Wet fabric is hung over an open fire after it is removed from the dye bath. Smoke is not a long-term fixative.

Best Fabric:

Cotton, Hemp, Wool – Other Textiles

Soda Ash, Sodium Carbonate, Washing Soda
Description:

Soda Ash is an alkali modifier derived from lakebeds or from kelp.

Common Uses:

Soda Ash is used in combination with copper to strengthen the green tone.

Soda Ash is used to raise the pH balance in some dye baths and help open the fabric fibers, allowing better penetration of the colorants.

Best Fabric:

Cotton

Amounts:

Soda Ash is added to a cooled dye bath at a rate of 1 ¼-teaspoon soda to 1-pound fabric.

Tannic Acid, Tannin
Description:
Tannin can occur naturally in plant products or you can purchase it as a fine powder for use in dyeing. Tannin is used on many vegetable fibers to help the mordant & colorant adhere better. Tannin can be used as a pre-mordant, as a mordant modifier, or as a stand alone mordant.

Common Uses:
Tannin helps to deepen the tone of colorants.

Tannin is used in combination with tin to enhance red tones.

Tannin is used a pre-mordant rinse to increase colorfastness when a metal based mordant will be used in the dye bath.

Best Fabric:
Cellulose Fibers, Cotton, Silk

Amounts:
Powdered tannin is used as a starting rate of 1 tablespoon of tannin to 1 pound of fiber simmered for up to 30 minutes.

Plant tannin is made by soaking 1 cup chopped plant parts in 1 gallon of water for 24 hours. The plants & water are then boiled for 1 hour. The plant parts will be strained from the liquid. The resulting fluid is used as a base for the dye bath. The finished fibers should be rinsed with vinegar.

Tartaric Acid
Description:
Tartaric acid is an acid modifier that is sometimes used as a stronger replacement for cream of tarter in dyeing.

Common Uses:

Tartaric Acid is a much stronger fabric protector and brightener than cream of tarter.

Best Fabric:
Silk, Wool

Amounts:
Tartaric Acid is used at a starting rate of 2 teaspoons powder to 1 pound of fabric.

Tin
Description:
Tin is a metal mined for use in manufacturing. It is also powdered for use in chemical processes including dyeing.

Common Uses:
Tin gives a brighter, more vibrant tone to colorants than other mordants.

Tin is frequently used to brighten the tones of colorants in the red, orange, and yellow spectrum and sometimes used to enhance purple tones.

Best Fabric:
Cotton, Satin, Silk, Wool

Amounts:
A good starting concentration for tin salts is ½ teaspoon per pound of fabric added before simmering the dye bath.

Tin should not exceed 3 teaspoons per pound of fabric.

Lower concentrations of tin will yield paler colors while higher concentrations of tin will give more depth to the final product.

Overuse:
Overuse of tin can makes fibers brittle.

Blends:

2 teaspoons Oxalic Acid or Tartaric Acid are used as a modifier for tin especially when dyeing silk and wool.

Fabric Considerations

Certain types of fabric take dye better than other fabrics and certain dye-mordant blends will work better on certain fabrics than they do on other fabrics. You should make notes defining exactly what you do with each mixture so you can make alterations or duplicate your processes. The instructions I have included are excellent starting points, but as you gain experience you will likely customize some of the processes to suit your personal needs and preferences.

The most common fabrics that you will dye are natural fabrics like wool, cotton, and silk.

Cellulose Fibers:
Cellulose fibers are fibers derived from plant materials and include cotton, hemp, linen, rayon, and other vegetable-based fabrics.

Protein Fibers
Protein fibers are fibers derived from animal materials and include angora, cashmere, leather, suede, and wool. Protein fibers need to be cleaned before dyeing.

Synthetic Fibers
Synthetic fibers are fibers created by people and include common items like nylon and rayon.

Dyeing

Once you have selected the mordant & mordant application method, you will begin the process of preparing your fibers and adding the dye.

You will use any pre-mordant you desire for your project. Review the mordant section to help you decide if a pre-mordant is recommended for your fabric type, plant products, and color you want to achieve.

You should have prepared the dye bath earlier. If you are using a meta-mordant or a mordant that is added directly to the dye bath, you will want to heat the dye bath just enough to dissolve the mordant in the fluid. Make certain the mordant is diffused throughout the bath to ensure you achieve even coloration.

I usually heat my fabric & dye bath. You can just soak the fabric if you prefer. Heating speeds the process somewhat and I like the way heated dye baths color. If you choose to heat the fabric & dye bath, place the mixture on the stove and bring it to a boil. Remove the mixture from the heat and allow it to cool naturally.

Allow the fabric to soak anywhere from one to twenty-four hours depending on the exact finish you want, colorant base you are using, and specific instructions relating to the mordant or colorant. It is important that you give the dye and mordant time to penetrate the fabric. The instructions for the fabric, mordant, and colorant you are using will help you determine the correct dyeing time. The visual review you complete as the dye bath soaks the fabric will help you fine-tune the timing. Trust your judgment because you have the best understanding of the finish you want for your project.

When the fabric has attained the color you desire, remove it from the dye bath. Remember that the final tone of the colorant will lighten when the fabric is rinsed and dried.

Wring out the excess dye. Most fibers should be rinsed through several changes of water. You will need to remove any excess colorant that has not penetrated the fibers.

If your results are not what you expected, you can over-dye the fabric with more of the same dye bath or try another dye bath to achieve an entirely new shade. The addition of a post-dye mordant can also help tone the hue to a more desirable shade.

You will apply any post-mordant rinse you desire. There are rinses that help to soften the fabric, brighten the tone, deepen the tone, change the color result, and even enhance the colorfastness of the dye. You should choose and apply the post-mordant that suits your project.

You can save your dye bath for reuse. A dye bath can be used as often as you wish until it no longer yields a desirable color. If you intend to store your dye bath for use on another day, you should place it in a cool storage area or in the refrigerator. A dye bath contains enough plant products that it will mold if left to sit for too long, especially in warm, moist conditions.

Remember to wear rubber gloves when handling the dye bath. Certain mordants can irritate the skin and all of the dye products will stain your skin and clothing.

Common Plant Colorants

Acai Berry
Euterpe oleracea

Acai Berry yields a natural purple color used as a cosmetic, culinary, or textile dye.

Acai is native to Central and South America. The Acai has adapted a specialized root system allowing it to grow well in areas prone to periodic flooding. It grows easily to zone 10 requiring a moist, humid environment and preferring bogs and swamps. Acai is propagated from seeds, often grown in a gelatin base and then transplanted to a constantly moist environment ranging from full sun to partial shade.

Agrimony, Church Steeples, Cocklebur, Stickwort
Agrimonia eupatoria

Agrimony is used as a textile and cosmetic colorant yielding a pale yellow color early in the year and a brassy yellow color later in the year. Mordant - Alum.

Agrimony is a hardy perennial native to Asia, Europe, and North America. It grows 3-4 feet tall and blooms yellow flowers in July and August that have been used a medicinal since the time of the Ancient Greeks. Agrimony is harvested by cutting the plant a few inches above the ground and air-drying the parts.

Agrimony is propagated by seed direct sown in the spring or fall or through division of the plant in the fall. It grows readily in sandy, loamy or heavy soils but prefers moisture and light shade. Agrimony will self-sew easily after yielding sweet scented flowers throughout the summer months.

Alder Buckthorn, Alder Dogwood, Arrow Wood, Black Dogwood, Frangula, Glossy Buckthorn
Rhamnus frangula

Alder Buckthorn bark yields a yellow dye product used as a textile dye.

Alder bark dye turns black when mixed with iron oxides.

Unripe Alder Buckthorn berries yield a green dye used as a cosmetic or textile dye.

Alder Buckthorn is a tall deciduous shrub native to Africa, Asia, and Europe and has been naturalized to parts of North America. It grows readily in wet soil associated with bogs and marshy zones. It prefers full sunlight but will grow in partial shade conditions and is considered an invasive species in some areas. It is sometimes cultivated as a hedgerow for its narrow, upright growth habit and feathery foliage and is hardy to zone 3. Alder Buckthorn is easily grown from seeds though they require 2-3 months cold stratification for optimal germination. It can also be propagated by spring cuttings or air layering.

Alfalfa, Lucerne, Luzerne
Medicago sativa

Alfalfa seeds yield a yellow toned colorant used as a cosmetic and textile dye.

Alfalfa is cultivated in many regions of the world as a food crop. Hardy to zone 5, it is not particular regarding soil composition and has been used to help fix nitrogen back into poor quality soils. It requires full sun but is not particular regarding soil or moisture conditions. Alfalfa is easily propagated by seed sown directly into the bed.

Alfalfa leaves and shoots are eaten as a raw or cooked vegetable or dried for use as a culinary additive, cereal or flour. Alfalfa seeds yield a yellow toned colorant used as a traditional cosmetic and textile dye. The seeds also yield a drying oil while the stems yield a fibrous material used in paper making.

Alkanet, Common Bugloss
Alkanna Tinctoria, Anchusa offinicinalis

Alkanet roots yield a red toned colorant commonly used as a culinary, cosmetic, or textile dye product.

Mordant choices and composition can alter the finished color toward brown or purple tones.

Alkanet root will yield the red color only if an oil-based bath is used. Water does not provide the same release of colorant.

Alkanet is a biennial native to Europe but has naturalized too much of North America where it is considered an invasive weed by some. Hardy to zone 5, it blooms from June through October with the seeds ripening in late summer or early fall. It is not particular regarding soil composition but does prefer good drainage and full sun. Alkanet is typically propagated by seed. Seeds can be started indoors during the spring or direct sown in the late fall for spring growth.

The flowers, leaves, and young shoots are eaten as a cooked vegetable. Alkanet roots yield a red toned colorant commonly used as a culinary, cosmetic, or textile dye product. Mordants and composition can alter the colorant toward brown or purple tones.

Almond, Bitter Almond, Sweet Almond
Prunus dulcis, Prunus amygdalus

Almond leaves yield a green toned colorant, the fruit yields a dark green-grey colorant and the roots yield a yellow colorant all used in textile dyeing,

Almond fruit yields a dark green-grey colorant and the roots yield a yellow colorant used in cosmetic, culinary, and textile dyeing.

Almond trees are native to Asia and Europe but have been naturalized in other parts of the world where they are grown as an ornamental plant or food crop. Almond is not particular regarding soil composition but does prefer full sun and consistent moisture. Almond can be propagated by cold stratified seed or by spring layering or cuttings taken throughout the growing season.

Amaranth, Love Lies Bleeding, Pilewort, Prince's Feather, Red Cockscomb, Velvet Flower
Amaranthus hypochondriacus

The whole Amaranth plant yields a yellow or green toned colorant used as a textile dye.

Amaranth seed produces a red toned colorant used as a cosmetic, culinary, and textile dye.

Amaranth is an annual common in tropical or temperate climates where it can be found growing in wastelands or cultivated as a grain food crop. It flowers in the mid summer and the seeds ripen in late summer to early fall. Each grain head produces thousands of seeds. Amaranthus is not particular regarding soil, growing well in sandy, loamy, or clay but it prefers good drainage and full to partial sun.

The leaves are harvested as a nutritious cooked or raw vegetable. The seeds are harvested and eaten raw or cooked, powdered for use as high-protein, high fiber flour, eaten as a cereal or popped in a manner similar to popcorn. Dye products obtained from the plant are used as a textile, culinary or natural product colorant.

American Chestnut, American Sweet Chestnut
Castanea americana, Castanea dentata

Chestnut bark yields a dark brown colorant used in dyeing textiles.

American Chestnut was once one of the most common trees in the eastern United States where the lightwood was harvested for use in making furniture, household goods and building products. Hardy to zone 4, it is not particular regarding soil composition but does prefer full to partial sun and consistent moisture though it will tolerate drought once established. The American Chestnut has been subject to blighting disease over the past decades greatly limiting their numbers. American Chestnut is easily propagated by seed but the seeds should not be stored since they become unviable if they dry out.

American Elder, Elderberry, Elder Flower, Sambucus, Sauco, Sweet Elder
Sambucus canadensis

The bark and leaves of the American Elder yield a dark brown to black colorant used as a dye for textiles and craftwork.

American Elder is a bush native to the United States but cultivated in other regions of the world. The plant will sucker to form dense thickets. It is also propagated by seed or cutting. It prefers full sun, but will tolerate partial shade and thrives in moist soil.

Annatto, Achiote, Bixin, Roucou, Lipstick Tree
Bixa orellana

Annatto seed coats yield an intense reddish-orange colorant used as a cosmetic and textile dye.

Annatto seeds yield a rich yellow colorant that is valued as a cosmetic and culinary dye.

The dye is water soluble and extracted by agitating the seeds in water.

Annatto is in actuality the extraction from the seeds of the Achoite tree. The tree is commonly called Annatto. Native to Central and South America, it has been naturalized to other tropical areas. Annatto is usually propagated by seed planted while still fresh. It is also possible to propagate Annatto by cuttings or air layering.

The seeds yield a yellow food colorant sometimes used for cosmetics and other items. The dye is water soluble and extracted by agitating the seeds in water. The pulp remaining after the colorant has been extracted from the seeds has been used as a poultry feed or ground fine and used as a flour substitute. The waxy residue left after the colorant has been removed from the seed coat is used as an insect repellant and has been used as a traditional treatment for treating intestinal parasites in animals. The oils are extracted for flavoring or coloring by covering a layer of seeds with oil and heating on high until the seeds pop. The seeds are removed and the resulting oil is used as a colorant additive in foods and cosmetics

Apricot
Prunus armeniaca

Apricot leaves yield a green toned colorant used as a textile dye and the fruits yield a dark grey colorant used as a cosmetic, culinary, or textile dye.

Apricot is a deciduous tree native to Asia, but naturalized in many regions of the world. Hardy to zone 5, it prefers sandy or loamy soil with good drainage, consistent moisture and full to partial sun. Apricot is typically propagated by seed but can also be propagated by spring layering or cuttings taken in the mid-summer.

Apricot seed oil is commonly used in perfumery, cosmetics, supplements, and commercial pharmaceuticals. Apricot leaves yield a green toned colorant and the fruits yield a dark grey colorant. The wood is hard and durable making it prized in small woodcraft, especially those related to tools.

Arbutus, Bearberry, Madrona, Madrone, Strawberry Tree
Arbutus menziesii

Arbutus bark yields a brown toned colorant used as a textile dye.

Arbutus is an evergreen tree native to North America and cultivated elsewhere. Hardy to zone 7, it prefers sandy to loamy soil, full to partial sun, and consistent moisture. Arbutus can be propagated by seeds sown out as soon as they are ripe, air layering, or cuttings taken in the early winter.

Arbutus bark yields a brown toned colorant and the bark has been used to make a rough fabric. Arbutus wood is used in watercraft, carving and furniture making.

Arrach, Goosefoot, Netchweed, Stinking Goosefoot, Stinking Motherwort, Wormseed
Chenopodium vulvaria

The whole Arrach plant yields a golden green colorant used as a cosmetic, culinary, and textile dye.

The color can be enhanced by using copper as a mordant.

Arrach is an annual herb native to Africa, Asia, and Europe and cultivated in other regions including North America. Hardy to zone 4, it is not particular regarding soil composition but does prefer full sun and consistent moisture.

Artichoke, Alcachofa, Alcaucil, Atichaut, Cardoon, Cynara, Kardone, Globe Artichoke
Cynara scolymus

The leaves of the artichoke plant yield a grey colorant used as a cosmetic, culinary, or textile dye.

Artichokes are a perennial plant hardy to zone 6. They flower in the late summer with the seeds ripening in early fall. While not particular regarding soil, the artichoke prefers moisture and full sun. Easily propagated by division of the suckers, artichoke is a commonly cultivated garden and commercial crop.

The flower buds are harvested before they open and the base is eaten as a raw or cooked vegetable. The young leaf stems are peeled and eaten like celery. The leaves are eaten as a cooked vegetable. The leaves of the artichoke plant yield a grey dye product used as a cosmetic, culinary, or textile colorant.

Asarabacca, Asari, Asarum, Coltsfoot, Hazelwort, Wild Ginger, Wild Nard
Asarum europaeum

The arial parts of the Asarabacca plant yield a bright green colorant used as a textile dye.

Asarabacca is a semi-evergreen groundcover native to Europe and cultivated in the United States. Hardy to zone 4, Asarbacca is accepting of a most soil composition but prefers semi-shade and moisture. Asarabacca spreads easily by runner and can be propagated by seed or division.

Ash, Bird's Tongue, Weeping Ash, White Ash
Fraxinus excelsior

Ash leaves yield a green colorant used as a textile dye and the bark is used as a fixative or tanning alternative.

The Ash tree can grow in many climates and is found across Europe and North America. Hardy to zone 4, Ash grows well in nearly any soil but does require consistent moisture to thrive. It is accepting of brackish water and pollution. The seeds are harvested in the spring before they are ripe and then sown immediately.

Ash wood is valued for fuel, tool making, and building products. The seeds are harvested, pickled in a salt vinegar solution and used as a seasoning or the oils extracted for use as culinary oil.

Bachelor's Buttons, Blue Bottle, Bluebonnet, Bluebow, Blue Cap, Blue Centaury, Cornflowers, Cyani Flowers, Hurtsickle
Centaurea cyanus

Bachelor Button's petals have been used for centuries as a natural blue culinary dye, especially in confections.

Bachelor Button petals yield a deep blue dye used as an ink alternative when mixed with alum.

Bachelor Button petals are mixed with a variety of mordants for dyeing textiles. Mordant – Alum.

Bachelor Buttons are an annual flowering plant native to Europe but naturalized over much of North America growing wild in woodlands, fields, and along roadways. They can thrive in nearly any soil but prefer good drainage and full sun. Bachelor Buttons are propagated by seed and will self-sow readily once a bed has been established.

Barberry, Agracejo, Berberry, Epine Vinette, Espino Cambron, Holly Leaved Barberry, Jaundice Berry, Mountain Grape, Oregon Grape, Pipperidge, Piprage, Sauderdorn, Sow Berry
Berberis vulgaris

Barberry roots, bark, and stem produce a yellow toned colorant used as a cosmetic or textile dye.

Barberry root tends to yield a more greenish gold while the bark yields a brighter yellow tone.

Barberry dye is very strong & colorfast. Mordant - Alum.

Barberry is indigenous to the United Kingdom and other parts of Europe but has naturalized throughout the eastern United States. Often cultivated as an ornamental plant growing 1-3 feet in height and width, Barberry is hardy to zone 3. It is not particular regarding soil composition or sunlight accepting semi or no shade. Barberry seeds should be sown as soon as they are ripe, cuttings of this years growth can be taken in the early fall and suckers can be removed in the spring.

Basil, Albahaca, Garden Basil, Munjariki, Surasa, Varvara
Ocimum basilicum

Basil tops yield a dark brown colorant used as a cosmetic, culinary, or textile dye. Mordant - Alum

Basil is a commonly cultivated spice herb that grows easily from seed. Hardy to zone 10, it prefers full sunlight, fertile soil, and steady moisture.

Bayberry, Bog Myrtle, Dutch Myrtle, Sweet Gale
Myrica gale

Bayberry yellow tips of the stems, seeds, and bark yield a yellow toned colorant used in textile dyeing.

Sweet Gale is a deciduous shrub native to Europe and North America where it is cultivated as an ornamental. It is not particular regarding soil composition but does prefer a moist, boggy base and light or no shade. Sweet Gale is propagated by seeds planted out as soon as they are ripe in the fall, cuttings taken at the end of the growing season or suckers divided early in the spring.

Beautyberry, American Beautyberry, French Mulberry, Sourberry
Callicarpa americana

Beautyberry fruits yield a purple toned colorant used as a cosmetic, culinary, or textile dye.

Beautyberry is native to the southeastern Unites States where it can be found growing wild in woodland settings or cultivated as an ornamental. Hardy to zone 7, Beautyberry is not particular regarding soil composition but does prefer full to partial sun and consistent moisture. It can be propagated by seeds sown in the spring, cuttings taken in late summer, or layering.

Beet, Garden Beet – Beta vulgaris craca, Sugar Beet
Beta vulgaris

Beet juice yields colorants ranging from deep red to dark purple used as a cosmetic, culinary, or textile dye.

Beets are a root vegetable with a number of varieties cultivated worldwide each carrying similar properties. Garden Beet, Sea Beet, and Sugar Beet have all been used in dyeing.

Beets are hardy to zone 5 and not particular regarding soil composition though they do require full sun and consistent moisture. They can be propagated by seed sown out in the spring.

Bigberry, Manzanita
Arctostaphylos glauca

Bigberry leaves yield a self-mordanting yellow to brown toned colorant used as a textile dye.

Bigberry is an evergreen shrub native to southwestern North America. Hardy to zone 8, it prefers sandy or loamy soil, full to partial sunlight and dry to moist conditions. It can be propagated by seeds planted as soon as they are ripe, air layering, or division of the plants in the spring.

Bilberry, Arielle, Black Whortles, Bleaberry, Brimbelle, Burnet Myrtle, Dyeberry, Huckleberry, Hurtleberry, Trackleberry, Whortleberry, Wineberry
Vaccinium myrtillus

Bilberry leaf and fruits yield a green toned colorant used as a textile dye.

Bilberry fruits yield a blue or black toned colorant used as a cosmetic or textile dye and in ink making.

Bilberry is a relative of the blueberry and grows well in Asia, Europe, and North America where it is a seasonally blooming shrub with interesting blue berries. Bilberry prefers damp, acidic soil and moderate sunlight. It can be propagated by seed planted after all chance of frost has passed, by cuttings taken mid-summer, sucker division in the spring, or through air layering.

Birch, Cherry Birch, White Birch
Betula pubescens

Birch bark yields a light brown to buff colorant used as a cosmetic or textile dye. Mordent Alum.

Birch roots yield colorants ranging in tone from red to purple-black used in dyeing textiles.

Birch is native to cold, northern climates and is a deciduous tree that grows well in many types of soil and sun conditions. Hardy in all zones, it flowers in the early spring with the seeds ripening in mid summer. Birch tolerates wind well and is sometimes grown as a windbreak. It can be propagated by seed sown indoors in the spring.

Bird Cherry
Prunus padus

Bird Cherry leaves yield a green colorant used as a cosmetic or textile dye.

Bird Cherry fruits yield a greenish gray colorant used as a textile dye.

Bird Cherry is native to North America where it can be found growing wild in moist open woods and upland areas. Hardy to zone 3, it is not particular regarding soil composition but does prefer good drainage and consistent moisture. It can grow in full sun, part sun, or semi-shade. Bird Cherry is propagated by seed planted in the late fall, softwood cuttings taken in the spring, hardwood cuttings taken in late winter, suckers divided just before spring, or air layering.

Bird's Foot, Trefoil
Lotus corniculatus

Birds Foot flowers yield an orange-yellow colorant used as a cosmetic or textile dye.

Birds Foot is perennial native to Africa, Asia, and Europe but has been cultivated in other areas as a wildlife plant. Hardy to zone 5, it is not particular regarding soil composition but does prefer good drainage and requires full sun. It can be propagated by seed soaked and then sown out after all danger of frost has passed.

Bitter Dock, Broad Leaved Dock, Dock Leaf, Kettle Dock, Round Leaved Dock
Rumex obtusifolius

Bitter Dock leaves yields a yellow colorant used as a textile dye.

The roots of the Bitter Dock yield a dark green to brown colorant used as a textile dye.

The heart of the Bitter Dock taproot yields a flesh-toned colorant.

Bitter Dock is native to Europe and naturalized in much of North America. It grows deep taproots that are difficult to remove once established. It is considered an invasive weed by some growing well in all types of soil, water, and sun conditions and resistant to cutting or trampling. Bitter Dock can be propagated by division or seed sown out in the spring.

Black Alder, Smooth Alder, Tag Alder
Alnus glutinosa

Black Alder is prized for yielding a wide range of dye products.

The bark of the Black Alder yields a red toned colorant used as a textile dye and to make ink.

Black Alder buds yield a green toned colorant used as a cosmetic or textile dye.

Fresh, green Black Alder wood yields a medium tan textile dye.

Black Alder bark and young shoots yield a yellow toned cosmetic or textile dye.

Black Alder shoots harvested as soon as they appear yield a dusky brown toned colorant.

The fruits of the Black Alder yield a dark red toned colorant used as a cosmetic or textile dye.

Black Alder is native to Asia, Europe, and North America. Hardy to zone 3, it prefers loamy or clay soil, full or partial sun, and moist or wet conditions. Black Alder grows quickly and has a reputation for fixing nitrogen into poor quality soil. It is cultivated by seeds sown as soon as they are ripe or cuttings taken in the late fall and planted in sandy soil during the winter.

Black Berry, Blessed Bramble, Bramble, Dewberry, Goutberry, Thimbleberry Rubi fruticosi radix

Blackberry shoots yield a gray toned colorant while the fruits yield tones ranging from medium red to strong purple used as a cosmetic, culinary, or textile dye.

The Blackberry is native to Europe and North America and has been naturalized to many parts of the world. It can be found growing in meadows, thickets, and cultivated gardens. Hardy to zone 6, it is not particular regarding sun condition or soil composition and will grow in poor quality soil. It does prefer moist, well-drained soil but cannot tolerate salt conditions. Blackberry is easily propagated by seed sown in the fall, cuttings taken mid-summer, or layering done in mid-summer.

Black Catechu, Black Cutch, Cachou, Cutch, Gambier, Mimosa Catechu Acacia catechu

Black Catechu bark is boiled to yield a caramel to coffee brown colorant used in cosmetic, culinary, and textile projects.

Black Catechu is thorny tree native to Asia and India. It is propagated in other regions by seed soaked in hot water and then sown indoors. It may also be propagated by cuttings taken in the spring.

Black Cherry, Black Choke, Chokecherry, Rum Cherry, Virginian Prune, Wild Cherry
Prunus serotina

The mixed berries and root of the Black Cherry or Chokecherry yields a reddish purple to bluish purple colorant used as a cosmetic, culinary, or textile dye.

Black Cherry leaves yield a green toned dye product used as a cosmetic or textile dye.

Black Cherry fruit alone yields a grayish green colorant used as a cosmetic, culinary or textile dye.

Black Cherry is deciduous tree native to North America and cultivated in Europe. Hardy to zone 3, it is not particular regarding soil composition but requires full sun and consistent moisture. It can be propagated by seed sown out as soon as it is ripe, air layering in the spring, or cuttings taken between spring and mid summer.

Black Cottonwood, Balsam Poplar, Western Balsam Poplar
Populus trichocarpa

Black Cottonwood leaf buds yield a yellow toned colorant used for dyeing wood and textiles.

Black Cottonwood is native to western North America. Hardy to zone 5, it is not particular regarding soil composition though it does prefer good drainage and consistent moisture, it will grow without them. It requires full sun and is propagated by seed sown as soon as it is ripe, cuttings taken in mid-summer, or from division of suckers taken early in the spring.

Black Currant, Cassis
Ribes nigrum

Black Current fruits yield a blue or light purple colorant used as a culinary, cosmetic, or textile dye.

Black Current is a berry native to Asia and Europe but cultivated in many other regions. Hardy to zone 5, it is not particular regarding soil composition but does prefer good drainage, consistent moisture, and full or partial sun. It is propagated by seed planted out in the fall as soon as they are ripe or cuttings taken in the late summer or early winter with a heel of old growth.

Black Eyed Susan, Bead Vine, Buddhist Rosary Bead, Crab's Eye, Gunja, Indian Bead, Jequirity Bean, Love Bean, Lucky Bean, Prayer Bean, Prayer Head, Precatory Bean, Rosary Pe, Seminole Bead, Weather Plant
Rudbeckia hirta

The leaf and stem of the Black Eyed Susan yields a gold to dull orange colorant used as a cosmetic or textile dye. Mordant – Alum

The flower head of the Black Eyed Susan give a khaki or olive green textile dye. Mordant – Alum

Black Eyed Susan is a perennial native to North America. Hardy to zone 4, it has bright gold blossoms throughout the summer. Black Eyed Susan is easily propagated by seed and is not particular regarding soil composition, but prefers full or part sun and consistent moisture. They can be found growing along roadsides or waste places and cultivated for ornamentals or as an erosion control plant. The seeds should be handled with care, as they are believed to be the source of the toxicity attributed to the Black Eyed Susan.

Black Locust
Robinia pseudoacacia

Black Locusts bark yields a yellow colorant used as a textile dye. It can be toned to different shades from bright yellow to burnished copper with the use of varying mordents.

Black Locust is native to the eastern North America and naturalized in areas of Africa, Asia, and Europe. Hardy to zone 3, it is not particular regarding soil composition and will grow in nutritionally poor soils. It requires full sun and dry to lightly moist soil. Black Locust can be propagated by seeds soaked in water and then sown in the early spring. Suckers can be divided from the mother plant during the dormant season.

Black Mulberry, Mulberry, Purple Mulberry
Morus nigra

Black Mulberry fruit yields a reddish purple to deep purple colorant used as a cosmetic, culinary, and textile dye.

Black Mulberry leaves yield a yellowish green colorant used as a textile dye.

Black Mulberry is believed to be native to Asia and has been cultivated in other regions of the world. Hardy to zone 5, it is not particular regarding soil composition but does prefer full or partial sun and moist soil. The seeds require 90 days cold stratification before planting. Black Mulberry can also be propagated by cuttings taken in mid-summer that contain both new growth and an old growth heel or through layering in the fall.

Black Raspberry, Blackcap, Raspberry, Raspberry Leaf, Thimbleberry
Rubus occidentalis

The berries of the black raspberry yield a colorant ranging from brown to purple depending on the ripeness of the berries and the strength of the dye bath. The berries are used as a cosmetic, culinary, or textile dye.

The roots and canes of the black raspberry yield a colorant ranging from purple to deep blue used as a textile dye.

Raspberry is native to Asia and Europe but grows well in most of Canada and the United States. It is not particular regarding soil composition but does prefer good drainage, consistent moisture, and partial shade. It is propagated by seed and is usually sown as soon as the seeds are ripe in the fall. It can also be propagated by cuttings taken in the mid-summer or layering in the fall.

Black Spruce
Picea mariana

The cones of the Black Spruce yield a yellowish-orange colorant used as a cosmetic or textile dye.

The Black Spruce is an evergreen tree native to northern North America. Hardy to zone 4, it is not particular regarding soil composition but does require full sun and boggy or consistently wet soil. Black Spruce can be propagated by seed sown out as soon as it is ripe, air layering or cuttings taken mid-summer through late fall.

Black Thorn, Blackthorn, Sloe, Wild Plum
Prunus spinosa

Blackthorn flower yields a yellow colorant used as a culinary, cosmetic, or textile dye.

The unripe Blackthorn berries are juiced for use as a burgundy to red colorant used as a cosmetic, culinary, or textile dye, indelible marker agent, and ink component.

The ripe berries yield a grayish green colorant used as a cosmetic, culinary or textile dye.

Blackthorn leaves yield a green toned colorant used as a textile dye.

Blackthorn shoots yield a stronger yellow colorant used as a textile dye. Mordant – Alum.

Blackthorn is a deciduous shrub native to Africa, Asia, Europe, and North America. Hardy to zone 4, it is not particular regarding soil composition but does prefer good drainage, light shade, and consistent moisture. It can be propagated by seeds sown out as soon as they are ripe, cuttings with a heel taken in mid summer, layering in the spring, or division of suckers at the end of the winter season.

Black Walnut, Jupiter's Nuts, Walnoot, Walnut
Juglans nigra

The ripe hulls of the Black Walnut yield a black colorant used as a cosmetic, textile, and woodcraft dye.

Black Walnut's unripe hulls yield a self-mordanting brown colorant. The unripe hulls have been used as a mordant for other dark toned dye projects.

Black Walnut cones and unripe seed coats yield a yellowish-orange colorant used as a textile dye.

The nuts, husks, leaf, stem, and bark of the Black Walnut yield a brown colorant. The hulls act as the mordant aiding the dyeing process. If iron is used, the dye turns black.

Black Walnut is a hardwood tree native to North America and the northern portions of Europe. Hardy to zone 4, it is not particular regarding soil composition but prefers good drainage, consistent moisture, and full or partial sun.

Blanket Flower
Gaillardia pinnatifida

Blanket flower heads yield a yellow to orange toned colorant used as a cosmetic, culinary, or textile dye.

Blanket Flower is a perennial that can be found growing wild in open fields. It is cultivated by seed in southern North America. Hardy to zone 8, it is not particular regarding soil composition but does prefer some sun and consistent moisture. Blanket Flower is sometimes propagated by root cuttings taken during the cold season months.

Bloodroot, Bloodwort, Coon Root, Indian Paint, Red Root, Sanguinaria, Sweet Slumber, Tetterwort
Sanguinaria canadensis

Bloodroot has a distinctive reddish-orange color and has been used since the times of the early Americans as a dye product.

Orange colors are achieved without a mordant, alum yields a rust tone, and tin gives a reddish pink colorant.

Bloodroot is a hardy perennial that grows to a height of 6-12 inches with white flowers that bloom in the spring. The root contains a natural red juice that looks like blood when the root is bruised or broken. It can be found in many parts of the United States especially on low hillsides and in forest borders. Hardy to zone 3, it is not particular regarding soil composition but does require full to partial sun and consistent moisture. Bloodroot is often propagated by seed sown in the spring, division in the early spring or late fall, or cuttings of shoots taken in the late spring.

Blueberry, Highbush Blueberry, Hillside Blueberry, Lowbush Blueberry, Rabbiteye
Vaccinium angustifolium

Blueberries yield a grayish blue toned colorant used as a cosmetic, culinary or textile dye.

Blueberries are found in many regions of the world where they are consumed as a food and harvested for use in traditional supplements. Hardy to zone 2, blueberry is not particular regarding soil composition but it does prefer full to partial sun and dry to moist soil. Blueberries can be propagated by seed sown out as soon as they are ripe or by air layering.

Borage, Bee Plant, Beebread, Borage, Borago, Borraja, Cool Tankard, Ox's Tongue, Talewort, Starflower
Borago officinalis

Borage flowers yield a blue toned colorant used as a cosmetic, culinary, or textile dye.

Borage is native to Europe and has naturalized in many other parts of the world including North America where it is considered an invasive weed in some regions. Hardy to zone 7, it is not particular regarding soil composition and can be easily propagated by seed. It will self-sow readily if given its own place in the garden.

Box Myrtle

Myrica nagi

Box Myrtle bark yields a yellow toned colorant used as a textile dye.

Box Myrtle is an evergreen tree native to Asia and cultivated in other regions as an ornamental. It is not particular regarding soil composition but does prefer full to partial sun and consistent moisture. Box Myrtle can be propagated by seeds sown out as soon as they are ripe, cuttings, or division of the suckers during the late winter.

Boj, Boxwood, Bush Tree
Buxus sempervirens

Boxwood leaves yield a burgundy colorant used in textile and hair-coloring agents.

Boxwood is native to Europe but has been naturalized to many other parts of the world where it is cultivated as an ornamental. Hardy to zone 5, it is not particular regarding soil composition but does prefer full to partial sun and dry to moist soil. Boxwood can be propagated by seed, spring cuttings, or air layering.

Bracken, Fern Bracken
Pteridium aquilinum

Bracken fronds yield a brown to green toned colorant depending on the mordant.

Bracken is a common fern native to much of the world, including the United States where it can be found growing wild in woodlands and open fields. Hardy to zone 4, it is not particular regarding soil composition, but does prefer full to partial sun and consistent moisture. Bracken is propagated by the sowing of spores directly on the surface of the soil and will self-sow readily if given its own place in the garden.

Brazilwood
Caesalpania echinata

Brazilwood shavings or dust are sprinkled with alcohol and then boiled to extract the red shaded colorant used as a textile dye or to create red ink.

Brazilwood is the common name of several tropical trees native to South America. All members yield a red toned colorant.

Scotch Broom
Cytisus scoparius

The flowers and green stems of the Cytisus scoparius known as the scotch broom yield colorants in tones ranging from yellow to yellow-green depending on the ripeness at the time of harvest. Mordant – Alum.

Broom stem bark yields a yellow to brown toned colorant.

Another species of broom the Genesta tinctoria is a shrub growing 2- 3 feet in height characterized by yellow flowers. All parts of the shrub are used as a colorant yielding a yellow tone. Mordant – Alum.

Scotch Broom is native to Europe and has been naturalized to parts of India, North America, and South America where it is cultivated for the evergreen shoots and golden flowers. Broom is considered an invasive species in some regions. Hardy to zone 5, it is not particular regarding soil composition but does prefer full to partial sun and consistent moisture. Scotch Broom can be propagated by seeds soaked and then sown as soon as they are ripe. It can also be propagated by fall layering or cuttings taken in the mid summer.

Buckhorn Plantain, Chimney-Sweeps, Headsman, Hoary Plantain, Lamb's Tongue, Ribgrass, Ribleaf, Ribwort Plantain, Ripplegrass, Soldier's Herb
Plantago lanceolata

The Buckhorn Plantain plant yields a golden brown colorant used as a cosmetic, culinary and textile dye.

Buckhorn Plantain is one of about 200 species of plantain found worldwide. Buckhorn is native to Asia and Europe. Hardy to zone 6, it is not particular regarding soil composition but does prefer full sun and consistent moisture. Buckhorn is propagated by seeds sown in the spring.

Buckwheat, Alforfon, Buchweizen, Grano Turco, Sarrasin, Silverhull
Fagopyrum esculentum

Buckwheat stems yield a blue toned colorant while the flowers yield tones of brown used as a cosmetic, culinary, and textile dye.

Buckwheat is believed to be native to Asia, but is commonly cultivated as a flour food crop in many regions. It is not particular regarding soil composition but does require full sun and prefers dry to moist conditions. Buckwheat is easily propagated by seeds sown out in the spring.

Bugleweed, American Water Hoarhound, Bugleweed, Egyptian Herb, Green Archangel, Gypsywort, Purple Archangel, Sweet Bugleweed, Water Bugle, Water Horehound, Wolf's Foot, Wood Betony
Ajuga Reptans

Bugleweed yields a natural black colorant used as a textiles dye, hair colorant, and sunless tanning agent.

Bugleweed is native to North America where it can be found growing wild in wetlands and cultivated elsewhere. Hardy to zone 5, it is not particular regarding soil composition, but does prefer full to partial sun and moist to wet conditions. Bugleweed can be propagated by seed sown out in the spring or by division in the spring or fall.

Butternut, White Walnut
Juglans cinerea

Butternut seed husks yield an orange to yellow toned colorant, the bark yields brown, the twigs yield tan tones and the young roots yield black colorants used as a cosmetic, culinary, or textile dye.

Butternut trees are native to eastern North America. Hardy to zone 4, they are not particular regarding soil composition but they do require full sun and consistent moisture. Butternut can be propagated by seeds sown out as soon as they are ripe.

Calafate, Magellan Barberry
Berberis microphylla

Calafate root and stem yield a yellow colorant that is used as a textile dye. Calafate has high tannin content and is self-mordant.

Calafate is an evergreen shrub native to South America. Hardy to zone 5, it is not particular regarding soil composition, but does prefer full to partial sun and dry to moist soil. Calafate can be propagated by seed sown out as soon as it is ripe or cuttings taken in mid summer.

Calendula
Bull Flower, Calendula, Gold Bloom, Holligold, Marigold, Mercadela, Pot Marigold, Zergul

Calendula flowers yield a colorant in tones of yellow, gold, and orange used as a cosmetic, culinary, or textile dye. Mordant – Alum

Calendula is an annual native to the Mediterranean but is cultivated as an annual garden plant in much of the world. Hardy to zone 6, it is not particular regarding soil composition but does prefer good drainage, full or part sun, and consistent moisture. Calendula is easy to grow from seed and will self-seed readily if given its own place in the garden.

Canadian Hemlock
Tsuga canadensis

The inner bark of the Canadian Hemlock yields a red colorant and the outer bark yields a reddish brown colorant used as a textile dye.

Canadian Hemlock is an evergreen tree native to North America. Hardy to zone 4, it is not particular regarding soil composition or sun, but does prefer consistent moisture. Canadian Hemlock can be propagated by seed cold stored and sown in the spring.

Canaigre, Arizona Dock, Canaigre, Ganagra, Tanner's Dock, Wild Rhubarb
Rumex hymenosepalus

Canaigre roots yield a colorant ranging from dark green to yellowish brown that is used as a self-mordanting textile dye.

Canaigre is native to Central America and southwestern North America. It is not particular regarding soil composition but does prefer full to partial sun and consistent moisture. Canaigre can be propagated by seeds sown in the spring or division.

Cankerroot, Chinese Coptis, Goldenthread, Mouth Root
Coptis trifolia
The leaves and stems of the Cankerroot yield a natural yellow colorant that has been used as a food & beverage dye, cosmetic colorant, or as a traditional textile dye.

Cankerroot is a bitter herb native to North America. Hardy to zone 2, it is not particular regarding soil composition, but does prefer partial sun and consistent moisture. Cankerroot can be propagated by seeds sown out as soon as they are ripe or by spring division.

Carob, Algarrobo, Garrofero, Locust Bean, St. John's Bread, Sugar Pods
Ceratonia siliqua

Boiled Carob pods yield a gray toned colorant used to dye cotton.

Carob is an evergreen native to Asia, Europe, and the Mediterranean but it has been cultivated in North America. It prefers sandy or loamy soils and is accepting of poor quality and nutrition. Carob requires full sun and dry to moist soil but is drought tolerant once established. It can be propagated by seeds soaked in warm water prior to sowing.

Carrot
Daucus sp.

The leafy tops of the carrot yield a green toned colorant and the roots yield shades of orange. Both are used in cosmetic, culinary and textile dyeing.

Carrot is a biennial native to Asia, eastern North America, and Europe. Hardy to zone 5, it is not particular regarding soil composition but does prefer full sun and consistent moisture. Wild Carrot is often found growing in untended fields and along roadsides. Carrot is easily propagated by seed and will self-sow readily if given its own place in the garden.

Cascara, Bitter Bark, Buckthorn, California Buckthorn, Dagrada Bark, Dogwood Bark, Persian Bark, Sacred Bark, Yellow Bark
Rhamnus purshiana

Cascara bark yields a green toned colorant used as a textile dye.

Cascara is native to the western United States and is cultivated in the US, Canada, and Africa. Hardy to zone 7, it is not particular regarding soil composition but does prefer full to partial sun and consistent moisture. Cascara can be propagated by seeds sown as soon as they are ripe, cuttings taken in mid-summer or layering.

Cedar, Ashe Juniper, Eastern Cedar, Pencil Cedar, Red Cedar, Red Cedarwood, Red Juniper, Texas Cedarwood, Virginia Cedarwood
Juniperus virginiana

Red Cedar wood yields a red toned colorant used as a textile dye or wood staining polish.

Red Cedar is native to the eastern parts of the United States. Hardy to zone 4, it is not particular regarding soil composition, but does prefer full sun and consistent moisture. It can be propagated by seed, but it is sometimes difficult to stimulate germination. Red Cedar is more often propagated by fall layering or cuttings of the current season's growth with a heel of mature wood taken late in the fall.

Centaury, Bitter Herb, Feverwort
Centaurium erythraea

Centaury flowers yield a greenish-yellow colorant used as a textile dye.

Centaury is native to Asia, Africa, and Europe and cultivated in the United States. It prefers sandy to loamy soil, full to partial sun, and dry to moist conditions. Centaury can be propagated by seeds sown out in the spring and will self sow readily if given its own place in the garden.

Chamomile
Chamaemelum nobile, Chamomilla recutita

Chamomile leaves produce a green toned colorant used in cosmetic, culinary and textile dyeing.

The flowers of another species of chamomile Anthemis tinctoria known as dyer's chamomile yield a yellow toned colorant. Mordant – Alum

Chamomile is native to Europe but has been naturalized as a landscape and herb in much of the word. Hardy to zone 4, it is not particular regarding soil composition but does prefer full or partial sun and consistent moisture though it can tolerate drought once established. Chamomile is easy to grow from seed and can be propagated by division in the spring or basal cuttings.

Chaste Tree, Agnocasto, Chaste Berry, Chasteberry, Hemp Tree, Monk's Pepper, Safe Tree, Vitex, Wild Pepper
Vitex agnus-castus

The leaves, seed, and root of the Chaste Tree yield a yellow toned colorant used as a cosmetic, culinary, or textile dye.

Chaste Tree is native to the Asia and the Mediterranean but is cultivated in many warmer regions. Hardy to zone 7, it prefers sandy or loamy soil with good drainage. Chaste Trees require full sun and dry to moist soil.

Cherry
Prunus sp.

The bark and branches of the cherry yield tones of brown and tans while the roots yield a blue to purple toned colorant used as a cosmetic or textile dye.

Cherry is naturalized in many regions where it is cultivated as an ornamental or for the fruits. Hardy to zone 3, it is not particular regarding soil composition but does prefer full to partial sun and consistent moisture. It can be propagated by seed, cuttings taken in mid-summer or layering in the spring. Suckers can be divided during the dormant season.

Chinese Foxglove, Di Huang, Gun Ji Whang, Rehmannia Root, Sheng Di Huang, Sho Jio, Shu Di Huang, To Byun

Rehmannia glutinosa

The flowers of the foxglove yield a colorant in a shade of pink toned beige used as a textile dye. Mordant – Alum.

Chinese Foxglove is a perennial native to Asia but it is also grown as an ornamental plant in much of North America. It prefers sandy or loamy soil with full or partial sun and consistent moisture. Chinese Foxglove can be propagated by seed or by root cuttings taken in the late spring.

Chitra, Barberry, Chitra, Tree Turmeric
Berberis aristata

Chitra root and stem yield a yellow colorant that is used as a textile dye. Chitra has high tannin content allowing it to act as a self-mordant.

Chitra is an evergreen shrub native to Asia. Hardy to zone 6, it is not particular regarding soil composition but does prefer full to partial sun and dry to moist soil. Chitra can be propagated by seed sown out as soon as it is ripe or by cuttings taken in the mid summer.

Cleavers
Barweed, Bedstraw, Catchweed, Cleavers, Cleaverwort, Eriffe, Gallium, Goose Grass, Gosling Weed, Grip Grass, Hayriff, Hedge Burs, Mutton Chops, Scratchweed
Galium aparine

Cleavers root yields a red toned colorant used as a textile dye.

Cleavers is annual native to Africa, Asia, Europe, North America, and South America. Hardy to zone 3, it is not particular regarding soil composition, sun conditions, or even moisture requirements. It is easily propagated by seed and will self-seed readily if given its own space in the garden.

Cocklebur
Clotbur, Cocklebur, Woolgarie
Xanthium strumarium

Cocklebur leaves yield a self-mordanting yellow toned colorant used in culinary, cosmetic and textile dyes.

Cocklebur seeds yield a blue self-mordanting textile dye.

Cocklebur is a hardy, self-seeding annual that can be found growing along wetlands in many parts of the world. Hardy to zone 7, it is not particular regarding soil composition but does prefer full sun and wet conditions.

Coffee, Expresso, Java, Mocha
Coffea arabica

Ground coffee beans yield a colorant in shades of tan to deep brown used as a cosmetic, culinary, or textile dye.

Coffee use dates back to the 1500's and coffee is one of the most common stimulants used in America today. The colorant parts of coffee come from the bean.

Coreopsis, Plains Coreopsis
Coreopsis grandiflora

Coreopsis tinctoria also known as Dyer's Coreopsis yields a gold, orange, or rusty red colorant. Mordant – Alum.

Another species Coreopsis grandiflora yields a gentle yellow colorant used as a cosmetic or textile dye. Mordant - Alum.

Coreopsis can also be toned to bronze using copper as a mordant.

Coreopsis is a perennial native to North America where it can be found growing wild along roads and in untended areas. It is not particular regarding soil composition but does prefer full sun and consistent moisture. Coreopsis can be propagated by seeds sown out in the spring.

Corn Poppy, Amapola, Copperrose, Coquelicot, Corn Rose, Cup Poppy, Headwark, Lalpost
Papaver rhoeas

Corn Poppy flowers yield a red colorant used as a cosmetic, culinary, or textile dye.

The corn poppy is native to Europe and Africa but it has been naturalized in North and South America. It is easily propagated by seed.

Cosmos, Yellow Cosmos
Cosmos sulphureus

The flower and stalk of the yellow cosmos yields an orange colorant used as a textile dye. Mordant – Alum.

Cosmos is annual flower growing 1-3 foot in height easily cultivated by seed and adapted to many regions of the world.

Couch Grass, Twitch Grass, Witch Grass
Agropyron repens

Couch Grass roots yield a grey toned colorant used as a textile dye.

Couch Grass is native to North & South America, Asia, Australia, and Europe. It is considered an invasive weed and grows readily in open grasslands, gardens, and other sunny locations. It is not particular regarding growing conditions and will self-sow readily if given its own place in the garden.

Cow Parsnip
Heracleum lanatum

Cow Parsnip roots yield a yellow colorant used as a cosmetic, culinary, or textile dye.

Cow Parsnip is native to the United States where it is considered an invasive weed by some. It is not particular regarding soil, sun, or moisture requirements and will self sow readily if given its own place in the garden.

Cranberries, Bearberry, Bog Cranberry, Cranberry, Craneberry,
Vaccinium macrocarpon

Cranberries yield colorants in shades of reds and pinks used as a cosmetic, culinary, and textile dye.

Cranberries grow in the acidic bogs of North America and are used in beverages, foods, dietary extracts, capsules, or tablets.

Crocus
Autumn Crocus, Colchicum, Crocus, Fall Crocus, Meadow Saffron, Mysteria, Naked Ladies, Upstart, Wonder Bulb
Colchicum autumnale

Crocus flowers yield a yellow toned colorant used as a textile dye.

Crocus is native to Europe and cultivated worldwide for its fall blooming flowers. Hardy to zone 5, it is not particular regarding soil composition but does prefer full to partial sun and consistent moisture. Crocus can be propagated by seeds sown out as soon as they are ripe but are more commonly propagated by division of the bulbs.

Dahlia
Dahlia rosea

Dahlia flowers and seeds yield a yellow to orange toned colorant used as a textile dye. Mordant - Alum

Dahlia is an ornamental flower cultivated for its intense colors. It is used as a dye product and the tuber has been eaten as a food in some cultures.

Dandelion, Blowball, Cankerwort, Clock Flower, Cochet, Dudhal, Endive, Fairy Clock, Fortune Teller, Irish Daisy, Lion's Tooth, Priest's Crown, Puff Ball, Swine Snout, Wild Endive
Taraxacum officinale

The dandelion flower yields a yellow colorant used as a cosmetic, culinary, or textile dye. Mordant – Alum.

The roots of the dandelion yield a natural orange-brown colorant used as a textile dye. Mordant – Alum

Dandelion is native to Asia, Europe, and North America where it is considered an invasive weed growing easily in a variety of sun, soil, and moisture conditions.

Day Flower
Commelina communis

The petals of the Day Flower yield a bright blue colorant used as a textile dye.

Day Flower is a perennial native to Asia but cultivated in other areas as an ornamental. Hardy to zone 7, it prefers sandy to loamy soil, full to partial sun and consistent moisture. Day Flower can be propagated by seeds sown out in the spring after all danger of frost has passed, cuttings or division.

Delphinium, Knight's Spur, Lark Heel, Lark's Claw, Larkspur, Lark's Toe, Staggerweed
Delphinium consolida

Delphinium flowers yield a deep blue toned colorant that has been used as an ink or as a textile dye. Mordant – Alum

Delphinium is a perennial that can be found growing wild at higher elevations worldwide. It is also cultivated as an ornamental.

Dewberry
Rubus caesius
Dewberry bush berries yield a grayish blue colorant used as a cosmetic, culinary, or textile dye.

Dewberry is native to Europe and North America. It resembles a raspberry but is typically a purple black color.

Digitalis, Dead Man's Bells, Digitale, Fairy Cap, Fairy Finger, Foxglove, Lady's Thimble, Lion's Mouth, Purple Foxglove, Scotch Mercury, Throatwort, Witch's Bells, Wooly Foxglove
Digitalis purpurea

Digitalis flowers yield a bright green toned colorant used as a textile dye.

Digitalis has an effect on the heart and caution should be used when handling the plant, plant dyes, or unwashed textiles dyed with digitalis.

Digitalis is native to Europe and cultivated as an ornamental in other areas. It is not particular regarding soil composition but does prefer full to partial sun and consistent moisture. Digitalis can be propagated by seed sown out after all danger of frost has passed.

Dock, Bloody Dock, Red Veined Dock
Rumex sanguineus

Bloody Dock roots yield a colorant ranging from dark brown to dark grey with a green undertone and it acts as its own mordant in textile dying.

Bloody Dock is a hardy perennial native to Africa, Asia, and Europe but naturalized in many other regions of the world where it can be found growing wild in untended areas. It is not particular regarding soil conditions but does prefer full or partial sun and consistent moisture.

Dogwood
Cornus sp.

Dogwood roots yield a reddish purple toned colorant used as a cosmetic or textile dye.

Dogwood bark yields a blue toned colorant while the fruits yield a greenish-blue tone used in textile dyeing.

Dogwood is a deciduous shrub native to eastern North America but it has been cultivated as an ornamental in other regions. Hardy to zone 5, it is not particular regarding soil composition but does prefer full to partial sun and consistent moisture. Flowering Dogwood can be propagated by seeds sown as soon as they are ripe, cuttings taken in mid summer or layering.

Dragon's Blood
Croton lechleri

Dragon's Blood fruits yield a red colorant used as a dye product and ink component.

Dragon's Blood is the resin of the Dragon Tree found in many tropical and sub-tropical regions around the world.

Dragons Blood, Sangre
Daemonorops draco

Dragon's Blood yields a red colorant used as a dye product and ink component.

Dragon's Blood is the resin of the Dragon Tree found in many tropical and sub-tropical regions around the world. The Dragon Tree is a type of palm hardy to zone 10b. It is not particular regarding sun conditions but does prefer a moist environment and rich soil.

Eastern Cottonwood
Populus deltoides

Eastern Cottonwood leaf buds yield a variety of dyes including green, purple, and red depending on the age of the buds with younger buds tending to green and the oldest buds entering the purple range.

Eastern Cottonwood is native to North America. Hardy to zone 2, it is not particular regarding soil composition but does require full sun and moist soil. It can be propagated by seeds sown as soon as they are rope, cuttings taken in the late fall, or division of the suckers in the spring.

Elder, Baccae, Black Elder, Elderberry, Ellanwood, Ellhorn, European Alder, Holunderbeeren, Sambucus, Sauco, Sureau
Sambucus sp.

Elder leaves yield a green colorant used in textile dyeing. Mordant – Alum.

Elder berries yield a colorant in a shade of blue-lilac used as a cosmetic, culinary, or textile dye. Mordant – Alum & Salt.

Elder roots yield a colorant in shades of red to orange used as a cosmetic or textile dye.

Elder bark yields a black toned colorant used in hair care and textile dying.

Elder is native to Europe and North America but has been cultivated in other regions. Hardy to zone 6, it is not particular regarding soil composition but does prefer full to partial shade and consistent moisture. Elder can be propagated by seed sown out in the spring or by cuttings taken in mid-summer. Suckers can be separated during the dormant season.

Mexican Elder
Sambucus mexicana

Mexican Elder fruits yield a black colorant used as a culinary, cosmetic, and textile dye product.

The stems of the Mexican Elder yield an orange-yellow colorant used as a textile dye.

Mexican Elder is a deciduous shrub native to wouthwestern North America and Mexico. It is not particular regarding soil composition but does prefer full or part sun and consistent moisture. Mexican Elder can be propagated by seed sown out as soon as it is ripe or cuttings taken in mid-summer. Suckers can be separated during the dormant season.

Elecampane
Alant, Aster, Elecampane, Elfdock, Elfwort, Horse Elder, Horseheal, Indian Elecampane, Scabwort, Velvet Dock, Wild Sunflower, Yellow Starwort
Inula helenium

Elecampane roots yield a colorant ranging from blue to purple depending on the age of the plant.

Elecampane is a perennial native to Europe and naturalized in many other areas of the world. It is not particular regarding soil composition but does prefer full or partial sun and consistent moisture. Elecampane grows easily from root cuttings or seed.

Elm
Ulmus sp.

Elm bark yield a coral toned colorant and the roots a brighter orange shade used as a textile dye.

Elm is a hardy tree native to Europe and naturalized in other parts of the world. Hardy to zone 6, it is not particular regarding soil composition but does prefer full to partial sun and consistent moisture. Elm can be propagated by seeds sown as soon as they are ripe, division of the suckers, or layering.

Epazote, Jesuit's Tea, Mexican Tea, Paico, Wormseed
Chenopodium ambrosioides

Epazonte is harvested whole and yields a green – gold toned colorant that is used as a self-mordanting textile dye.

Epazote is native to Central & South America. Hardy to zone 8, it is not particular regarding soil composition but does require full sun and consistent moisture.

Eucalyptus
Blue Gum Blue Mallee, Gully Gum, Gum Tree, Red Gum, Stringy Bark Tree, Sagandhapara
Eucalyptus globulus

Young Eucalyptus leaves yield a self-mordanting yellow colorant that tones to tan with the mordent alum.

The young Eucalyputs shoots yield tones of grey to green and the young bark yields a darker green. Mordant copper sulfate.

Eucalyptus is native to Australia but is cultivated in many other parts of the world. Hardy to zone 9, it is not particular regarding soil composition but does prefer full sun and moist to wet conditions. Eucalyptus can be propagated by seeds sown after all danger of frost has passed. If sown indoors, seedlings should be transplanted to their permanent location as soon as the second set of leaves appear.

European Chestnut, Husked Nut, Jupiter's Nut, Sardian Nut, Spanish Chestnut, Sweet Chestnut
Castanea vulgaris

Chestnut seed has been ground fine and used as a bleaching agent for cloth.

The Chestnut tree is native to much of Europe and has been naturalized to other parts of the world including the United States.

Fennel, Biri Sanuf, Bitter Fennel, Carosella, Fennel, Hinojo, Sweet Fennel, Wild Fennel, Xiao Hui Xiang
Foeniculum vulgare

The whole plant of the bronze fennel yields a clear yellow tone colorant used as a cosmetic, culinary, and textile dye. Mordant - Alum.

Fennel is an annual plant native to the Mediterranean but is cultivated worldwide as it is easily grown from seed in rich soil with plenty of sun and moderate moisture. It grows to a height of 3-6 feet and has yellow flowers that bloom in the summer months. Fennel should be grown away from other plants since it may inhibit their growth.

Fir - Douglas
Pseudotsuga menziesii

Douglas Fir bark yields a light brown toned colorant used as a self-mordanting textile dye.

Douglas Fir is a fast growing, wind resistant evergreen native to North America. Hardy to zone 7, it is not particular regarding soil composition, but does require full sun and moist to wet conditions. Douglas Fir can be propagated by seeds sown out as soon as they are ripe.

Fumitory, Beggary, Earth Smoke, Fumaria, Fumus, Hedge Fumitory, Vapor, Wax Dolls
Fumaria officinalis

Fumitory flowers yield a yellow toned colorant used as a cosmetic or textile dye.

Fumitory is an annual native to Europe but has been naturalized to parts of North & South America. Hardy to zone 5, it prefers sandy or loamy soils, full to partial sun and consistent moisture. Propagated by seed, Fumitory will self-seed readily and is considered an invasive weed by some.

Gamboge, Brindle Berry, Camboge, Gambodia, Gamboge, Gutta Gamba, Tom Rong
Garcinia hanburyi

Gamboge yields an orange to mustard yellow toned colorant used as a textile dye.

Gamboge is native to Europe where the gum resin is harvested from the bark of mature trees for use as a dye product and traditional supplement.

Garlic Mustard
Alliaria petiolata

Garlic Mustard yields a yellow toned colorant used as a cosmetic, culinary, and textile dye.

Garlic Mustard is native to Africa and Asia but has been naturalized to Europe and North America where it is considered an invasive species by some. It is not particular regarding soil composition but does prefer full shade and consistently moist or wet soil. It is propagated by seed and will self-seed readily if given its own place in the garden.

Gipsywort, European Bugleweed, Gypsyweed, Water Horehound
Lycopus europaeus

Gipsywort juice yields a black colorant that is permanent on wool, fades over time on skin & hair, and will require a mordant for other purposes.

Gipsywort is native to Europe and has been naturalized in other areas where it can be found growing in water or in boggy areas. Hardy to zone

5, it is not particular regarding soil composition but does prefer full to partial sun and moist to wet conditions.

Goldenrod, Aaron's Rod, Woundwort
Solidago virgaurea

Goldenrod flowers and stalks yield bright yellow to gold tone colorants used as a textile dye. Mordant – Alum.

The whole plant can provide a brown toned colorant for textile dyeing. Mordant – Chrome.

Goldenrod is a perennial wildflower that grows up to 5 feet in height. It is native to Asia, Europe, and North America where it can be found growing wild in fields and along roads.   Hardy to zone 5, it is not particular regarding soil composition or moisture but does prefer full to partial sun. Goldenrod can be propagated by seeds sown out in the spring and will self-sow readily if given its own place in the garden. Clumps can also be divided in the spring or fall.

Goldenseal, Eye Balm, Eye Root, Goldenroot, Ground Raspberry, Indian Dye, Indian Plant, Indian Turmeric, Jaundice Root, Orange Root, Turmeric Root, Wild Curcuma, Yellow Indian Pain, Yellow Puccoon, Yellow Root
Hydrastis canadensis

The roots and stalk of the goldenseal yield a yellow colorant used as a textile dye product.

Goldenseal is a perennial native to Eastern North America. Hardy to zone 3, it can be found growing wild in part of the US or cultivated in many supplement gardens. It is not particular regarding soil composition but does prefer full to partial shade and consistent moisture. It can be propagated by seed planted out as soon as they are ripe or by divisions of larger clumps in the fall.

Good King Henry
Chenopodium bonus-henricus

Good King Henry is harvested whole and yields a green – gold toned colorant that is used as a self-mordanting textile dye.

Good King Henry is native to Europe and North America where it can be found growing in fields, pastures, and untended areas. Hardy to zone 5, it is not particular regarding soil composition but does require full sun and consistent moisture. It can be propagated by seed but germination is sometimes difficult so it is more commonly propagated by spring division.

Grape, Calzin, Draksha, Grape Seed, Grapeseed, Red Vine, Uva
Vitis vinifera

Grape leaves and roots yield a yellow colorant used as a textile dye.

The fruits of the grape yield a colorant in tones of blue to purple used as a cosmetic, culinary, or textile dye.

The roots of another species of grape the wild grape, Vitis riparia roots yield a purple colorant.

The leaves, branches, and fruits of the grape have been used in traditional supplements, dyes, and culinary products since the time of the Ancient Greeks. Supplement grapes are deciduous climbing vines native to Europe and cultivated in many other regions of the world. Hardy to zone 6. they are not particular regarding soil composition but do prefer full to partial sun and dry to moist soil. Grape is easily propagated by seed, cuttings of the current season's growth taken in mid-winter or layering throughout the year.

Green Alder
Alnus viridus

Green Alder bark yields a red to brown toned textile dye depending on the age and mordant combination.

Green Alder is a deciduous shrub native to eastern North America. Hardy to zone 4, it is not particular regarding soil composition but does prefer full to partial sun and consistent moisture. Green Alder can survive in poor quality soil and is sometimes use to fix nitrogen back into the dirt. Green

Alder can be propagated by seeds sown as soon as they are ripe or cuttings taken in the late fall after the leaves have dropped.

Green Osier, Agoda Dogwood
Cornus alternifolia

The roots of the Green Osier yield a dark brown colorant used as a hair & textile dye.

Green Osier is a deciduous shrub native to eastern North America. Hardy to zone 3 it is not particular regarding soil composition but does prefer good drainage, full sun, and consistent moisture. It can be propagated by seed sown out as soon as it is ripe, cuttings taken in mid summer with a heel of the previous year's growth, or air layering in the summer.

Dyer's Greenwood, Green Weed, Wood Waxen
Genista tinctoria

Dyer's Greenwood yields bright yellow colorant with the flowers and shoots giving a better tone than the rest of the plant. Mordant – Alum

Dyer's Greenwood is mixed with woad to produce a green colorant.

Dyer's Greenwood is native to Europe and has been naturalized to the United States where it can be found growing wild in untended areas. Hardy to zone 2, it prefers sandy to loamy soil and requires full sun and consistent moisture. Dyer's Greenwood can be propagated by seeds sown indoors as soon as they are ripe. Seed germination is somewhat difficult. It is more commonly propagated by cuttings taken in the mid summer.

Grindelia, Gum plant, Gumweed, Tarweed
Grindelia robusta

Grindelia flowers yield a yellow toned colorant and the seedpods yield a green toned colorant used in textile dyeing.

Grindelia is native to Central and North America. Hardy to zone 7, it prefers sandy to loamy soil, full sun, and dry to moist conditions. Grindelia can be propagated by seed sown in the spring and will self sow readily if given its own place in the garden.

Han Lian Cao, False Daisy
Eclipta prostrata

Han Lian Cao yields a black toned colorant used as a natural dye product for the hair, skin, and textiles.

Han Lian Cao is a perennial native to Asia. Hardy to zone 8, it is not particular regarding soil composition but does prefer partial shade and moist to wet conditions. Han Lian Cao can be propagated by seeds sown out in the spring.

Hazel, Aveleira, Cobnut, Hazel Nut, Noisettes
Corylus avellana

Hazelnut bark, roots, and nuts yield colorants in shades of brown to tan. The bark and roots are used primarily for textiles while the nuts are also used as a cosmetic or culinary dye.

The Hazel is a deciduous tree native to Europe but cultivated in many other parts of the world. Hardy to zone 4, it is not particular regarding soil composition but does prefer full to partial sun and consistent moisture.

Heartsease, Field Pansy, Heart's Delight, Heart's Ease, Johnny Jump In, Ladies Delight, Pansy, Pennsee, Viola, Wild Pansy
Viola tricolor

Hearts Ease flowers yield colorants ranging from yellow to aquamarine depending on the flower selected and mordant choice.

Hearts Ease is a member of the viola family native to Asia and Europe and cultivated in other regions. Hardy to zone 4, it is not particular regarding soil composition but does prefer full to partial sunlight and consistent moisture. It is propagated by seed sown out as soon as it is ripe and over-wintered or by division in the fall.

Heartseed Walnut, Japanese Walnut
Juglans ailanthifolia cordiformis

The nuts of the Heartseed Walnut yield a yellow toned colorant that is used as a self-mordanting textile dye and sometimes as a cosmetic or culinary dye.

The hulls of the Heartseed Walnut yield a colorant in brown tones used as a skin, hair, and textile dye product.

Heart Seed Walnut is a deciduous tree native to Asia and cultivated in other regions of the world. Hardy to zone 4, it is not particular regarding soil composition but does prefer good drainage, full sun, and consistent moisture. It is propagated by seeds sown as soon as they are ripe or by removal of the suckers early in the growing season.

Heather, Culluna, Ling
Calluna vulgaris

Heather flower and leaves yield a golden orange colorant used as a textile dye. Mordant – Alum.

Heather is an evergreen shrub like plant growing 12-18 inches in height. It is native to Europe but has been naturalized to other parts of the world including eastern North America. Heather prefers sandy or loamy soil, full or partial sun and consistent moisture though it will tolerate some dryness. It can be propagated by seed sown out as soon as it is ripe, cuttings taken in the late summer or divisions of larger clumps taken anytime during the growing season.

Henna, Alcanna, Egyptian Privet, Henna, Mehndi, Mendee, Mignonette Tree, Reseda, Smooth Lawsonia
Lawsonia inermis

Henna powders can be colorless or finished in shades of red or black and are frequently used as colorants in cosmetics.

Henna is a shrub or tree native to the Middle East and cultivated in other tropical and sub-tropical regions.

Henna powders can be colorless or finished in shades of red and are frequently used as colorants in natural care products. Henna is harvested, dried, and powdered for use in external applications or as a traditional supplement tea up to 3 times daily though the FDA has only approved Henna as a hair colorant.

Herb Paris, One Berry, True Lover's Knot
Paris quadrifolia

Herb Paris berries yield a red toned colorant and the leaves yield a yellow colorant used as a cosmetic, culinary, or textile dye.

Herb Paris is native to Europe and cultivated in other parts of the world as an ornamental. Hardy to 6, It prefers sandy to loamy soil, full to partial shade and consistent moisture. Herb Paris can be propagated by seeds sown as soon as they are ripe or division of mature plants.

Herb Robert, Crow's Foot, Dove's Foot, Dragon's Blood, Mountain Geranium, Red Robin, Robert Geranium, Stinky Bob, Storksbill, Wild Crane's Bill
Geranium robertianum

Herb Robert yields a brown colorant used as a hair, skin, or textile dye.

Herb Robert is native to Africa, Asia, and Europe and naturalized to North and South America. Hardy to zone 6, it is not particular regarding soil composition but does prefer full to partial sun and dry to moist soil. Herb Robert is propagated by seed sown in the spring and will self-sow readily if given its own place in the garden.

Hibiscus, Gongura, Guinea Sorrel, Jamaica Sorrel, Karkade, Red Sorrel, Red Tea, Roselle, Sour Tea, Sudanease Tea
Hibiscus sabdariffa

Yellow Hibiscus flowers yield a yellow toned colorant while red or purple Hibiscus flowers yield a dusky red toned colorant used as a cosmetic or textile dye.

Hibiscus is an annual cultivated in many warmer regions as an ornamental and as a container plant in other places. Hardy to zone 10, it is not particular regarding soil composition but does prefer full sun and consistent moisture. Hibiscus is propagated by bulbs planted out in the spring or by division and separation of the bulbs prior to winter storage.

Hollyhock, Althea Rose, Malva, Rose Mallow
Alcea rosea

The lighter toned flowers of the Hollyhock yield colorants in tones ranging from yellow to golden brown used as a cosmetic or textile dye. Mordant – Alum

The darker toned flowers of the hollyhock yield colorants in tones ranging from lilac to deep mauve used as a cosmetic or textile dye. Mordant – Alum.

A red extract of hollyhock flowers has been used as litmus.

Hollyhock is a perennial shrub believed to be native to Asia but naturalized in many other regions to the point where its origin is unclear. Hardy to zone 6, it is not particular regarding soil composition but it does require full sun and dry to moist soil. Hollyhock can be propagated by seed sown out in the spring or in the fall as soon as they are ripe. It can also be propagated by division after flowering, root cuttings taken during the winter, or basal cuttings taken during the growing season.

Hoopesii, Helenium, Herb of the Wolf, Owl's Claw, Yerba del Lobo
Hymenoxys hoopesii

Hoopesii flowers yield a yellow toned colorant used as a textile dye.

Hoopesii is a hardy perennial native to the southwestern United States where it can be found growing wild in grassy and untended areas. Hardy to zone 3, it is not particular regarding soil composition but does prefer full to partial sun and consistent moisture. Hoopesii can be propagated by seed sown out in the spring, cuttings taken in mid-summer or division.

Hops, Houblon, Lupulin

Humulus lupulus

Hops leaves and flower heads yield a brown toned colorant used as a cosmetic, culinary, and textile dye.

Hops are native to Asia & Europe but are cultivated in North America. Hardy to zone 5, it is not particular regarding soil composition but does prefer full or partial sun and moist soil though it can tolerate drought once established. Hops can be propagated by seed sown out in the spring or by cuttings taken early in the season.

Hops leaves and flower heads yield a brown toned colorant and the female fruits yield oil used in perfumery. The stems are used to make hemp like cording and are sometimes used to make cloth.

American Hornbeam, Hornbeam
Carpinus caroliniana

Hornbeam bark yields a yellow colorant used as a textile dye.

Hornbeam is a deciduous tree native to North America.

Horse Chestnut, Buckeye, Chestnut, White Chestnut
Aesculus hippocastanum

Horse Chestnut, Sweet Chestnut, and other chestnuts are used to make dusky parchment or to give gray tone to fabric. Used primarily as a leather dye it is often incorporated as a base colorant in other dyeing.

Horse Chestnut bark yields a yellow toned colorant used as a cosmetic, culinary, and textile dye.

Horse chestnut trees are native to Greece but have been naturalized throughout much of the northern hemisphere. Hardy to zone 3, it is not particular regarding soil composition but does prefer full to partial sunlight and consistent moisture. The Horse Chestnut can be propagated by seeds sown out as soon as they are ripe.

While the Horse Chestnut is sometimes called a buckeye, it should not be confused with the Ohio Buckeye.

Horsetail, Bottle Bush, Dutch Rushes, Horse Herb, Paddock Pipes, Pewterwort, Souring Rush, Shave Grass, Spring Horsetail, Toadpipe
Equisetum arvense

Horsetail stems yield a pink toned colorant used as cosmetic or textile dye.

Horsetail is native to Europe and Asia but has been naturalized in other regions. It is not particular regarding soil composition but does prefer full or partial sun and consistent moisture. Horsetail is propagated by spores sown out as soon as they are ripe or division at any time during the growing season. It will self-sow readily if given its own place in the garden.

Horsetail – Dutch Rush, Horsetail, Scouring Rush
Equisetum hyemale

Dutch Rush Horsetail stems yield a light pink colorant used as a cosmetic or textile dye.

Dutch Rush Horsetail is native to Europe and Asia. It can be propagated by spores but will spread readily if given its own space in the garden.

Hyacinth, Bai Qu, Hyacinth - Orchid
Bletilla striata

Hyacinth flowers yield a blue toned colorant used as a cosmetic or textile dye.

Hyacinth is native to Japan but is also a common ornamental cultivated worldwide for its spring flowers. Hardy to zone 7, it prefers loamy soil with good drainage, partial light and consistent moisture. It is propagated by seed sown as soon as it is ripe or division in the spring. New growth can also be stimulated by wounding the bulb.

Hydrangea, Hortensia, Mountain Hydrangea, Seven Barks, Sevenbark, Smooth Hydrangea, Wild Hydrangea
Hydrangea arborscens

Hydrangia flowers yield a light green colorant used as a cosmetic or textile dye. Mordant - Copper and Alum.

Hydrangea is native to eastern North America. Hardy to zone 3, it is not particular regarding soil composition but does prefer full to partial sun and consistent moisture. Hydrangea can be propagated by seeds sown in the spring, cuttings taken at the end of the growing season, division of the suckers during the dormant season or layering.

Impatiens, Balsam Weed, Jewel Weed, Jewelweed, Orange Jewelweed, Silverweed, Slipper Weed, Spotted Jewelweed, Orange Balsam, Touch Me not, Wild Balsam, Wild Celandine
Impatiens capensis

The entire Impatiens plant, but especially the flowers, yield a yellowish orange colorant used as a textile dye.

Impatiens is native to North America. Hardy to zone 2, they are not particular regarding soil composition but do prefer part shade and consistent moisture. Impatiens can be propagated by seed sown in the spring.

Indian Kamilla, Apuyot, Kamilla, Pikal, Rohini, Spoonwood, Tagusala
Mallotus philippensis

Kamilla glands & hair yield a red colorant used as a cosmetic or textile dye.

Indian Kamilla is native to Asia, Australia, and India where the oils are used as a wax product, cosmetic ingredient, or varnish. The glands & hairs are powdered as a dye product.

Indian Madder, Madder, Manjistha, Tamaralli
Rubia cordifolia

Indian Madder stems & root yield a red colorant used as a cosmetic or textile dye.

Indian Madder is a perennial native to Africa, Asia, and Europe. Hardy to zone 6, it is not particular regarding soil composition but does prefer partial shade and consistent moisture. Indian Madder can be propagated by seeds sown when they are ripe or division.

Indian Mulberry, Ba Ji Tian, Canarywood, Cheese Fruit, Mengkudu, Noni, Ura, Wild Pine
Morinda citrifolia, Morinda officinalis

Indian Mulberry fruits yields a red, orange, or yellow colorant depending on the combination of plant parts used and age of the plant. Indian Mulberry is used in cosmetic, culinary, or textile dyeing.

Indian Mulberry is a small shrub like tree native to the tropical regions of the Pacific Ocean. A popular supplement item, the leaves and fruit can be purchased as a fresh natural food product, tea, juice, or powder.

Indian Spinach, Creeping Spinach, Malabar Spinach, Phooi Leaf, Red Vine Spinach
Basella alba

Indian Spinach leaves yield a green colorant used as a traditional cosmetic, culinary, or textile dye.

Indian Spinach fruits yield a red toned colorant used as a cosmetic and textile dye product or mixed with lemon juice for use as a culinary colorant.

Indian Spinach is a semi-succulent vine native to Africa and Asia. Hardy to zone 8, it is not particular regarding soil composition but does require full sun and consistent moisture. Indian Spinach can be propagated by seed sown out in the spring or by stem cuttings taken during the growing season.

Indigo, Dyer's Indigo
Indigofera tinctoria

Indigo yields a highly valued blue dye that is used by many cultures worldwide to produce tones ranging from sky to midnight blue. Indigo is also over dyed with yellow to produce an array of green shades.

Indigo is a perennial shrub growing up to 3 feet in height and blooming during the summer months with a range of violet colored flowers.

Indigo – Wild, American Indigo, Baptista, False Indigo, Horsefly Weed, Indigo Broom, Rattlebush, Wild Indigo, Yellow Indigo
Baptisia tinctoria

Wild Indigo is related to Dyer's Indigo but has smaller concentrations of blue toned colorant. It can be used in larger quantity to achieve the same tones as Dyer's Indigo.

Wild Indigo is a perennial native to eastern North America. Hardy to zone 5, it prefers sandy or loamy soil and has the ability top add nitrogen back into nutritionally poor areas. It does require full sun and prefers consistent moisture. It can be propagated by seed sown out as soon as it is ripe and it self-seeds readily. Wild Indigo can also be propagated by division of larger clumps early in the growing season.

Iris, Yellow Flag, Yellow Iris
Iris pseudacorus

Yellow Iris flowers yield a brilliant yellow colorant used as a cosmetic or textile dye.

Yellow Iris root yields a brown colorant without a mordant and a black colorant with an iron sulphate mordant. The root colorant is often used to make ink.

Deep purple iris flowers yield a dark blue to purple colorant. Mordant – Alum.

Yellow Iris is a scented perennial native to Africa, Asia, and parts of Europe but it is also cultivated as an ornamental in many regions of the world. Hardy to zone 5, it prefers sandy or loamy soil, full to partial sun, and wet conditions or water habitats. Yellow Iris can be grown by seeds sown out as soon as they are ripe or division early in the spring.

English Ivy, Gum Ivy, Lierre Grimpant, True Ivy, Woodbind
Hedera helix

English Ivy stems yield a brownish yellow colorant used as a textile dye.

The leaves yield a black toned colorant used as a textile dye or to hair colorant.

English Ivy is an evergreen climber native to Asia and Europe but has been naturalized to many areas of the world. Hardy to zone 5, it is not particular regarding soil composition or sun conditions but does prefer moist or wet soil. English Ivy can be propagated by seed soaked until the coat bursts. It can also be propagated by cuttings taken in the mid summer or layering. The plants will self-propagate through layering.

Jerusalem Artichoke
Earth Apple, Jerusalem Artichoke, Sunroot
Helianthus tuberosus

Jerusalem Artichoke roots yield yellow toned colors used as a cosmetic, culinary or textile dye.

Jerusalem Artichoke is a hardy plant native to eastern North America. Hardy to zone 4, it is easily grown from sliced tubers in a manner similar to propagating a potato. Jerusalem Artichoke is not particular regarding soil composition but does prefer full sun and consistent moisture.

Joe-Pye Weed, Gravel Root, Kidney Root, Purple Boneset, Tall Boneset
Eupatorium purpureum

Joe Pye Weed fruits yield a pink or red colorant used as a textile dye.

Joe-Pye Weed is perennial native to eastern North America. Hardy to zone 4, it is not particular regarding soil composition but does prefer full or partial sun and consistent moisture. It can be propagated by seed sown in the spring or division in the late spring.

Joseph's Coat, Bhaji, Callaloo, Chinese Spinach,
Amaranthus tricolor

Joseph's Coat yields a yellow to green toned colorant used as a textile dye.

Joseph's Coat is a tricolor annual native to South America but cultivated in other parts of the world as an ornamental. Hardy to zone 5, it is not particular regarding soil composition but does prefer full sun and consistent moisture. Joseph's Coat is easily propagated by seed sown out in the late spring or cuttings taken throughout the growing season.

Joshua Tree
Yucca brevifolia

The root of the Joshua Tree yields a red to reddish black dye depending on the time of harvest with the darker colors becoming more prevalent as the plant ages.

Joshua Tree is an evergreen native to the southwestern United States. The leaves are used as a weaving, fiber product and the roots have been used as a traditional dye or soap substitute.

Knotweed, Allseed, Anjubar, Armstrong, Beggarweed, Bird's Tongue, Birdweed, Centinode, Cow Grass, Crawlgrass, Doorweed, Hogweed, Knotgrass, Pigrush, Pigweed, Red Robin, Sanguinaria, Sparrow Tongue
Polygonum aviculare

Knotweed aerial parts yield a yellow to green toned colorant used as a textile dye.

Common Knotweed is native to Asia and Europe where it can be found growing wild in wastelands and untended areas. Hardy to zone 5, it is not particular regarding soil composition but does prefer full to partial sun and consistent moisture. Knotweed can be propagated by division or seeds sown in the spring and will self sow readily if given its own place in the garden.

Kukui Nut, Candlenut, Indian Walnut, Varnish Tree
Aleurites moluccanus

The inner bark of the Kukui Nut tree yields a reddish brown colorant used in cosmetics, ink, and textile dyes.

Kukui nut has been naturalized over nearly every tropical and sub-tropical region of the world. The nut is eaten as a cooked culinary additive and the oils have been extracted from the nuts for use as a lamp oil or varnish component. The ripe nuts are pounded into paste and used as a soap alternative. The inner bark of the Kukui Nut tree yields a reddish brown colorant used in cosmetics, ink, and textile dye.

Labrador Tea
Ledum groenlandicum

Labrador leaves yield a brown colorant used as a cosmetic, hair colorant or textile dye.

Labrador is an evergreen shrub found growing naturally in northern climates. It is not particular regarding soil composition or light but does prefer moist or wet soil. It is propagated by seed, cuttings taken in mid-summer or layering in the fall.

Lady's Bedstraw, Cheese Rennet, Cheese Renning, Curdwort, Galliet Juane, Maid's Hair, Petty Mugget, Yellow Cleavers, Yellow Galium
Galium verum

The roots of Lady's Bedstraw yield a colorant in tones ranging from brick red to coral. Mordant – Alum.

The flowers of Lady's Bedstraw yield a colorant in tones ranging from yellow to dull gold. Mordant – Alum

Without a mordant, the extracted colorants are used as a culinary or cosmetic dye.

Lady's Bedstraw is a perennial native to Asia and Europe. Growing 2-3 feet in height and blooming in the early summer with yellow flowers, it is hardy to zone 3 and not particular regarding soil composition. It does prefer full to partial sun, good drainage, and moist soil. Lady's Bedstraw can be propagated by seed and will self-seed readily. It can also be divided throughout the growing season.

Lady's Mantle, Lion's Foot, Nine Hooks, Silerkraut, Stellaria
Alchemilla vulgaris

Lady's Mantle flowers yield a yellow colorant used as a textile dye.

Lady's Mantle is a perennial indigenous to many regions of the world, growing 10-18 inches in height and blooming in early summer with yellow flowers. It grows easily from seed, cuttings, and division and is a pretty and beneficial component in the garden.

Lady's Thumb, Jesusplant, Red Leg, Redshank, Smartweed
Polygonum persicaria

Lady's Thumb yields a yellow colorant used as a textile dye. Mordant – Alum

Lady's Thumb is native to Europe but has been naturalized over much of the United States where is can be found growing wild in damp, shaded areas. Hardy to zone 5, it is not particular regarding soil composition but does prefer partial shade and moist to wet conditions. Lady's Thumb can be propagated by seeds sown in the spring.

Larkspur
Delphinium exaltatum

Larkspur flower heads yield a blue toned colorant used as a cosmetic or textile dye.

The whole Larkspur plant can be used to achieve a dusky yellow colorant used as a textile dye.

Lavender
Lavandula angustifolia, Lavandula officinalis

Lavender mixed with lemon juice has been used to make a bright pink colorant used as a cosmetic, culinary or textile dye.

Lavender is native to the Mediterranean and was used in supplements and ceremonial treatments in ancient Egypt, Greece, and Rome. Hardy to zone 5, it is cultivated worldwide for use as a traditional aromatherapy, supplement tea, or extract. Lavender is not particular regarding soil composition but does prefer full sun, well-drained soil, and consistent moisture. It can be propagated by seed sown out in the spring or by cuttings taken in the mid-summer with a heel of the previous year's growth.

Lilac
Syringa vulgaris

Lilac flowers & leaves yield a green to brown colorant used as a cosmetic or textile dye.

Lilac twigs yield a dull yellow colorant used as a textile dye.

Lilac is a deciduous flowering shrub native to Europe but is cultivated as an ornamental in many other places including North America. Hardy to zone 5, it is not particular regarding soil composition but does prefer full sun and consistent moisture. Lilac can be propagated by seed but is more reliably propagated by suckers divided out at the end of the dormant season or layering in the spring.

Lily of the Valley, Constancy, Confallaria, Ladder to Heaven, Lily, May Bells, May Lily, Muguet, Our Lady's Tears
Convallaria majalis

The whole Lily of the Valley plant yields a pale green toned colorant used in textile dyeing.

Lily of the Valley is native to Asia, Europe, & North America where it is cultivated as an ornamental. Hardy to zone 3, it is not particular regarding soil composition or sun conditions but does prefer heavy moisture. Lily of the Valley can be propagated by seeds sown out as soon as they are ripe or division during the growing season.

Logwood, Bloodwood
Haematoxylon campechianum

Logwood yields gray-lavender to blue purple toned colorant used as a textile dye.

Alum as a mordant creates the popular logwood gray color.

Logwood is native to North America, Mexico, and Central America and is known as the spiny tree.

Loosestrife, Blooming Sally, Long Purples, Purple Loosestrife, Purple Willow Herb, Rainbow Weed, Spiked Loosestrife, Willow Sage
Lythrum salicaria

Loosestrife flowers yield an edible dye product that varies in shade depending on the base being colored.

Loosestrife is a native to Asia, Australia, and North America.

Madder, Bengal Madder, Dyer's Madder, Garanca, Indian Madder, Robbia
Rubia tinctoria

The roots of the madder yield a very strong textile dye in varying shades of red ranging from red-orange to red-brown depending on the strength of the dye bath. Mordant – Alum.

Madder is a perennial growing up to 2 feet in height and blooming with tiny pale yellow flowers throughout the season. It is native to Europe, Asia, and Africa but cultivated in other regions. Hardy to zone 6, it prefers sandy to loamy soil, full to partial sun and dry to moist conditions. Madder can be propagated by seeds sown as soon as they are ripe or through division.

Magnolia, Beaver Tree, Ho No Ki, Holly Bay, Hou Po, Indian Bark, Japanese Whitebark, Red Bay, Red Magnolia, Swamp Laurel, Swamp Sassafras, Sweet Bay, White bay, White Laurel, Xin Ye, Hua
Magnolia officinalis

Magnolia flower yields a yellow toned colorant used as a cosmetic or textile dye.

Magnolia is a scented ornamental native to Asia and cultivated in many warmer areas of the world. It is not particular regarding soil composition but does prefer good drainage, full to partial sunlight, and consistent moisture. Magnolia can be propagated by seeds sown out as soon as they are ripe or by spring layering.

Maidenhair Fern, Five Finger Fern, Maiden Fern, Rock Fern, Venus Hair Fern
Adiantum capillus-veneris

Maidenhair yields a dark brownish black colorant that is used in natural hair darkening products and as a textile dye.

Maidenhair is native along the Atlantic Coast of Europe and North America. Hardy to zone 9, it is not particular regarding soil composition but does prefer full to partial shade and consistent moisture. Maidenhair Fern is propagated by spores sown as soon as they are ripe or division.

Mallow, Common Mallow, High Mallow, Tall Mallow, Malva
Malva sylvestris

Common Mallow leaves & roots yield a yellow colorant used as a cosmetic, culinary, or textile dye.

Mallow leaves and seeds can be blended to create cream and green toned colorants used in cosmetics, culinary, and textiles.

Common Mallow is native to Africa and Asia but has naturalized to Europe and North America. Hardy to zone 5, it is not particular regarding soil composition but does prefer full or partial sun and consistent moisture. Common Mallow is easily propagated by seed and will self-sow readily.

Mallow – Little, Cheeseweed, Little Mallow
Malva parviflora

Little Mallow leaves & roots yield a yellow colorant while the leaves and seeds can be blended to create cream and green toned colorants used as a cosmetic, culinary, or textile dye.

Little Mallow is native to Africa and Asia but is now common to fields & untended areas in most regions of the world. It is easily propagated by seed and will self-sow readily if given its own place in the garden.

Maple
Acer sp.

Maple bark & roots yield a blue to purple colorant used as a textile dye.

Maple leaf buds yield a reddish-brown color and dried leaves yields shades of brown to black used as a cosmetic or textile dye.

The inner bark yields a purple toned colorant used as a textile dye.

Maple is a common tree found growing wild or cultivated in many regions of the world. Hardy to zone 3, it is not particular regarding soil composition but does prefer full to partial sun and consistently moist soil. Maple can be propagated by seed sown out as soon as it is ripe, air layering or cuttings of new growth taken in the spring.

Silver Maple
Acer saccharinum

Silver Maple bark yields a colorant in tones of dark brown to blue black depending on the mordant. The colorant is used as a textile dye or ink product.

Silver Maple is a type of Maple native to eastern North America. Hardy to zone 3, it is not particular regarding soil composition but does prefer full to partial sun and consistently moist soil. Silver Maple can be propagated by seed sown out as soon as it is ripe, air layering or cuttings of new growth taken in the spring.

Maritime Pine
Pinus pinaster

Maritime Pine needles yield a greenish toned colorant used as a textile dye.

Maritime Pine is native to Africa and Europe but is cultivated in other regions for use in commercial and traditional supplement preparations. Hardy to zone 8, it is not particular regarding soil composition but does prefer full sun and consistent moisture. It can be propagated by seed sown out as soon as it is ripe or cuttings taken from young trees during the summer months.

Marsh Marigold, Bull's Eyes, Horse Blobs, Kingcups, Leopard's Foot, Meadow Root, Palsy Root, Water Blobs, Water Dragon
Caltha palustris

Marsh Marigold flowers yield a yellow colorant used as a culinary, cosmetic, and temporary textile dye.

Marsh Marigold is native to most temperate regions. Hardy to zone 3, it is not particular regarding sol composition but does prefer full to partial sun and consistent moisture. Marsh Marigold can be propagated by seeds sown as soon as they are ripe or division.

Marsh Woundwort, All Heal, Panay, March Woundwort
Stachys palustris

Marsh Woundwort yields a yellow toned colorant used as a paint or textile dye.

Marsh Woundwort is native to Asia and Europe. Hardy to zone 5, it is not particular regarding soil composition but does prefer full to partial sunlight and moist to wet soil. It is commonly cultivated in warm region bog gardens. Marsh Woundwort is propagated by seeds sown out in the spring or spring division.

Meadowsweet, Bridewort, Dolloff, Dropwort, Lady of the Meadow, Meadow Wort, Mead Wort, Quaker Lady, Queen of the Meadow, Ulmaria
Filipendula ulmaria

Meadowsweet roots yield a dark brown colorant and the aerial parts yield a yellow toned colorant used as a cosmetic or textile dye.

Meadowsweet is native to Asia and North America and can be found growing in boggy areas. Hardy to zone 2, it is not particular regarding soil composition but does prefer full to partial sun and moist to wet soil. Meadowsweet can be propagated by seeds sown as soon as they are ripe or division.

Motherwort, Chinese Motherwort, Lion's Ear, Lion's Tail, Mother's Wort, Throw Wort
Leonurus caridiaca

Motherwort leaves yield a drab green colorant used as a textile dye.

Motherwort is perennial native to Europe and naturalized in North America. It is not particular regarding soil composition but does prefer full or partial sun and consistent moisture. Motherwort is easily propagated by seed and will self-sow readily but can also be propagated by division.

Mountain Alder, Grey Alder
Alnus tenuifolia

Mountain Alder bark yields a red to brown toned colorant used as a textile dye.

Mountain Alder is native to western North America. Hardy to zone 2, it is not particular regarding soil composition and will tolerate heavy, poor quality soils. Mountain Alder has been used to fix nitrogen back into the soil. It does prefer full to partial sun and consistently moist to wet conditions. Mountain Alder can be propagated by seeds sown out as soon as they are ripe or cuttings taken in the late fall after the leaves have dropped from the branches.

Mountain Laurel, Broad Leafed Laurel, Calico Bush, Lambkill, Laurel, Mountain Ivy, Rose Laurel, Sheep Laurel, Spoon Laurel, Spoonwood
Kalmia latifolia

Mountain Laurel leaves yield a pale yellow colorant used as a cosmetic or textile dye.

Mountain Laurel is a relative of the blueberry native to the eastern United States. Hardy to zone 4, it is not particular regarding soil composition but does prefer full to partial sun and consistent moisture. Mountain Laurel can be propagated by seed sown in the early spring, layering, or cuttings taken from young plants.

Mulberry, Red Mulberry, White Mulberry
Morus

Unripe Mulberry berries yield a red to orange colorant used as a cosmetic, culinary, or textile dye.

Ripe Mulberries yield a rich shade of purple used in cosmetic, culinary, and textile dyeing.

The white bark of the mulberry tree yields a cream colorant used as a textile dye. Mordant - Alum.

White Mulberry is native to Asia and Red Mulberry is native to the United States but all species are cultivated worldwide.

Mullein, Adam's Flannel, Beggar's Blanket, Blanket Herb, Candleflower, Candlewick, Duffle, Feltwort, Flannel Leaf, Flannelflower, Great Mullein, Woolen
Verbascum thapsus

The whole Mullein plant with the fine hairs removed yields a yellow to green colorant used as a culinary or textile dye.

Mullein flowers yield a yellow toned colorant used as a textile dye or hair colorant.

Mullein is native to Africa, Asia, and Europe but has been naturalized to North America where it is considered an invasive weed by some. Hardy to zone 3, it is not particular regarding soil composition or moisture but does require full sun. Mullein can be found growing wild in untended areas or propagated by seeds sown out in the spring.

Myrobalan, Arjuna, Axjun, Argun, Bahera, Balera, Hara, Harad, Haritaki, He Zi, Indian Almond, Kalidruma, Tropical Almond, Vibhitaki
Terminalia chebula

Myrobalan is a versatile colorant often used to alter the tone of another dye.

Myrobalan is used as a mordant before dyeing black or brown fabric.

Myrobalan extract over dyed with indigo makes a deep teal color.

On its own, Myrobalan gives a brownish yellow to light buff color.

Myrobalan is native to India and grows primarily in the Himalayas.

Nettle, Bichu, Nettle, Stinging Nettle, Utica
Urtica dioica

The entire Nettle plant can be used to create a natural colorant in shades of yellow, gold, and beige depending on the strength of the bath and age of the plant. Mordant – Alum

Nettle leaves and stems yield a green toned colorant used as a textile dye.

Nettle is a perennial native to Asia and Europe but has been naturalized throughout North America. Hardy to zone 3, it is not particular regarding soil composition but does prefer full or partial sun and consistent moisture. Stinging nettle is easily propagated by seed sown out in the spring and will self-sow readily if given its own place in the garden. It can also be propagated by division at any time during the growing season.

Nutmeg, Jaatipatree, Jiaphal, Jatikosha, Jatipatra, Jatipatri, Javitri, Mace, Macis, Muscadier, Muskatbaum, Mace, Ron Dau Kou
Myristica fragrans

The nutmeg seed yields tones of golden brown used in cosmetic, culinary, and textile dyeing.

Oak, Durmast Oak, English Oak, Pedunculate Oak, Sessile Oak, Stave Oak, Stone Oak, Tanner's Oak,
Quercus robur

Oak bark & root yield a colorant in tones of brown to black most frequently used for tanning leather.

Shelled Acorns nuts yield tan to pinkish beige colorants while the whole acorn yields tones of browns & tans used as a cosmetic or textile dye.

Oak Galls are used to make a black dye or ink product. The colorant is more rust colored when mixed with Iron Oxide.

Oak trees are found in many regions of the world. Oak Gall is the Gall produced on the Oak by gall wasps that lay their eggs in the leaf buds of the Oak Tree.

Onion
Allium cepa

The skins of onions yield shades of bright brown, reddish brown, orange brown or yellow depending on the age and quality of the skins. Onion skin dye is used as a cosmetic, culinary or textile dye. Mordant – Alum.

Cream of Tarter added to the mix yields tones shading toward yellow.

Onions are native to Asia but have been cultivated worldwide for culinary use. Hardy to zone 5, Onion prefers sandy or loamy soil, full sun and consistent moisture. It is easily propagated by seed sown out in the late spring.

Orach, Saltbush
Atriplex hortensis

Orach seeds yield a blue colorant used as a cosmetic, culinary or textile dye.

Orach is native to many regions of the world thriving in both desert and marine environments. It is easily propagated by seed sown in the spring.

Orris Root, Bearded Iris, Daggers, Flag, Flaggon, Flag Lily, Fliggers, Florentine Iris, Gladyne, Iris, Jacob's Sword, Liver Lily, Myrtle Flower, Poison Flag, Purple Flag, Queen Elizabeth Root, Shegg, Snake Lily, Water Flag, White Dragon Flower, Wild Iris, Yellow Flag, Yellow Iris
Iris germanica

Orris root yields a black colorant used as a culinary, cosmetic, or textile dye and the flowers yield a blue toned textile dye.

Orris is native to Europe and naturalized to the United States. Hardy to zone 5, it is not particular regarding soil composition but does prefer full to partial sun and consistent moisture. Orris can be propagated by seeds sown as soon as they are ripe or division of the clumps.

Papaya, Melon Tree, Paw Paw
Carica papaya

Papaya fruits yield a yellow toned colorant used as a traditional cosmetic, textile, and culinary dye.

Papaya is native to Central, North, and South America and cultivated as a food crop in other regions. It prefers loamy soil with good drainage, consistent moisture, and full sun.

Papaw, Paw Paw, Papaw
Asimina triloba

Papaw fruits yield a yellow toned colorant used as a cosmetic, culinary or textile dye.

Papaw is native to the southeastern United States. Hardy to zone 5, it prefers well-drained, loamy soil, full sun, and consistent moisture. Papaw can be propagated by seed sown out as soon as it is ripe or air layering during the growing season.

Paprika, African Bird Pepper, African Chilies, African Pepper, Aji, Bird Pepper, Capsicum, Cayenne Pepper, Chili, Garden Pepper, Goat's Pod, Grain's of Paradise, Green Pepper, Hot Pepper, Hungarian Pepper, Louisiana Long Pepper, Mexican Chilies, Red Pepper, Sweet Pepper, Tabasco Pepper, Zanzibar Pepper
Capsicum annum

Paprika fruits yield a pastel yellow to pale orange toned colorant used as a cosmetic, culinary, and textile dye.

Paprika refers to a family of commonly cultivated peppers typically grown by seed sown out in the spring in full sun and moist conditions.

Pasqueflower, Anemone, Easter Flower, Meadow Anemone, Meadow Windflower, Pasque Flower, Passe Flower, Pulsatilla, Wind Flower

Pulsatilla vulgaris

Pasqueflower flowers yield a green colorant used in textile dyeing.

Pasqueflower is native to Asia and Europe, but has been naturalized in other parts of the world. Hardy to zone 4, it is not particular regarding soil composition, but does require full sun and consistent moisture though it can tolerate drought once established. Pasqueflower is propagated by seed sown out as soon as it is ripe and will self-sow readily if given its own place in the garden. It can also be propagated by summer division. Be mindful of flagging from root disturbance.

Passion Fruit
Grenadilla

Passion Fruit skins yield a brown to tan toned colorant used as a cosmetic or textile dye. Mordant Alum.

Peach
Prunus persica

Peach leaves yield a yellowish green toned colorant used as a cosmetic, culinary, and textile dye.

Peach trees are native to Asia but have been naturalized in many other regions where the fruit is cultivated as a food.

Peach – Desert, Desert Almond, Desert Peach
Prunus andersonii

Desert Peach fruits yield a grey-green colorant and the leaves yield a green toned colorant used as a cosmetic, culinary, or textile dye.

Desert Peach is native to western North America. It is not particular regarding soil composition but does prefer full to partial sun and consistent moisture. Desert Peach can be propagated by seeds sown as soon as they are ripe, cuttings taken in mid-summer or layering.

Pearly Everlasting, Western Pearly Everlasting

Anaphalis margaritacea

Pearly Everlasting flowers, stems, and leaves yield gold to green toned colorant used as a cosmetic, culinary and textile dye.

Pearly Everlasting is a perennial native to North America where it can be found growing wild in moist meadows and along the banks of rivers and streams. Hardy to zone 3, it prefers sandy to loamy soil, full to partial sun and dry to moist conditions. Pearly Everlasting is easily propagated by seeds sown out as soon as they are ripe and will self-sow readily if given its own place in the garden. It can also be propagated by division at any time during the growing season.

Peppermint, Black Peppermint, Bo He, Brandy Mint, Lamb Mint, Mentha, Mint, Mint Balm, Sentebon, White Peppermint
Mentha x piperita officinalis, Mentha x piperita vulgaris

Peppermint leaves yield a khaki green colorant used as a cosmetic, culinary, or textile dye.

Peppermint is a cross between water mint and spearmint native to the Mediterranean but naturalized throughout much of the world. Hardy to zone 3, peppermint is a hardy perennial that spreads rapidly by runner in nearly any soil, sun, and water conditions and may become an invasive weed.

Perilla, Shiso
Perilla frutescens

The leaves of the purple perilla plant yield a purple colorant used as a culinary or textile dye.

Perilla is a perennial herb native to Asia, Europe, and North America. It is an easily propagated member of the mint family that spreads by runner. Perilla is considered an invasive weed by some.

Phellodendron, Cork Bark, Cork Tree
Phellodendron amurense

Phellodendron bark yields a yellow colorant used as a culinary and textile dye.

Phellodendron is a tree native to Asia and should not be confused with the cultivated houseplant commonly called Philodendron.

Pine
Pinus sp.

Pine cones yield a brown to tan colorant used as a textile dye and the needles yield a green toned dye.

The bark creates a self-mordanting medium brown colorant.

Numerous varieties of pine exist and they are naturalized in many parts of the world. Hardy to zone 2, Pine prefers sandy to loamy soil but is not particular regarding soil nutrition. It prefers full or partial sun and consistent moisture. It is propagated by seed sown out as soon as it is ripe or by cuttings of young trees taken in the spring. Removing the needles form the branches to be cut a month prior to taking the cuttings sometimes helps with propagation.

Poke Root, Indian Poke
Phytolacca acinosa

Poke fruits yield a red toned colorant used as an ink or textile dye.

Poke is native to eastern Asia and has naturalized in other parts of the world including North America. Hardy to zone 7, it is not particular regarding soil composition but prefers full to partial sun and consistent moisture. Poke can be propagated by seed sown in the spring or division of the clump early in the growing season.

Plum
Prunus americana

Plum tree bark and roots yield a reddish purple color and the roots alone yield a salmon color used as a textile dye. Mordant - Alum.

Pomegranate, Dadima
Punica granatum

The dried rind of the pomegranate fruit produces colors ranging from deep yellow to greenish-yellow tones. The age of the fruit affects the final color of the dye with the less ripe fruits containing more green tones. Iron mordant gives a deep mossy green color.

The flowers and unripe fruit rind of the pomegranate yield a red to reddish black toned colorant used in cosmetics, textile dyeing, and ink.

The root bark yields a deep black colorant with high tannin content giving it the ability to act as a self-mordant.

Pomegranate is native to Africa, China, and India and has been naturalized to parts of California and Arizona. Hardy to zone 9, it is not particular regarding soil composition or moisture but does prefer full sun. Pomegranate is easily propagated by seed, mature cuttings, layering, or by division of the suckers.

Prickly Ash, Hercules Club, Pepper Wood, Toothache Bark, Yellow Wood
Zanthoxylum rhetsa

The leaves of the prickly ash yield a pale yellow colorant used as a textile dye. Mordant – Alum.

Prickly Ash pods yield a colorant in shades of red to purple used as a culinary or textile dye.

Prickly Ash is a deciduous shrub found growing along coastlines.

Quebracho
Schinopsis lorentzii

The bark of the Quebracho tree has a distinctive red color making it useful as a natural dye product. It is most suitable for dyeing silks and cellulose fibers and creates a lovely peach to brownish rose color.

Quebracho is native to Argentina, Brazil, and Chili.

Rabbitbrush
Ericameria nauseosa

The bark of the rabbitbrush shrub yields a greenish colorant used as a textile dye.

Rabbitbrush flowers yield a golden colorant used as a textile dye.

Rabbitbrush is a shrub native to western North America and cultivated elsewhere as an ornamental or as a forage plant. It is not particular regarding soil composition and can thrive in poor quality soil and water conditions. It can be propagated by seed and will self-sow readily if given the right conditions. Rabbitbrush can also be propagated by division of suckers and by layering in the spring.

Giant Ragweed, Horseweed, Ragweed
Ambrosia trifida

Ragweed flowers and plant sap yield a red to yellow colorant depending on the age of the plant. It is used as a cosmetic or textile dye.

Ragweed is considered a weed found growing throughout untended areas of eastern North America but it was cultivated by the Native Americans as an oil producing plant and food product. It is not particular regarding soil composition but does prefer full or partial sun and consistent moisture. It is easily propagated by seed and self-sows readily if given its own location.

Ragwort, Groundsel, Life Root
Packera aurea

Ragwort flowers yield a yellow toned colorant used as a textile dye. Mordant – Alum.

The colorant tends toward a brown to orange tone when no mordant is used.

Ragwort is considered a weed and can be found growing in untended areas of North America. Hardy to zone 3, it is not particular regarding soil composition but does prefer full to partial sun and moist to wet conditions. Ragwort can be propagated by seeds and will self sow readily if given its own place in the garden. Ragwort can also be propagated by division or root cuttings taken in the spring.

Raspberry, Framboise, Raspberry Leaf
Rubus idaeus

Raspberry fruit yields a blue to purple colorant used as a culinary, cosmetic, or textile dye.

Raspberry can be found in many regions of the world and is native to much of North America. Though Raspberry can thrive in a variety of conditions, it does prefer partly shaded areas and consistent moisture for optimal growth.

Chinese Raspberry, Korean Bramble, Raspberry – Chinese
Rubus coreanus

Chinese Raspberry fruit yields a matte blue colorant used as a culinary, cosmetic, or textile dye.

Chinese Raspberry is native to Asia. Hardy to zone 6, it is not particular regarding soil composition but does prefer full to partial sun and consistent moisture. It can be propagated by seed cold stored and then sown in the spring or division of the suckers.

Red Alder
Alnus glutinosa

Red Alder bark yields a red to brown toned colorant used as a textile dye.

Red Alder is native to western North America. Hardy to zone 2, it is not particular regarding soil composition and is tolerant of heavy, poor quality dirt. Red Alder has been used to fix nitrogen back into the soil. It does prefer full to partial sun and consistently moist to wet soil. Red Alder can be propagated by seeds sown out as soon as they are ripe or cuttings taken in the late fall after the leaves have dropped from the branches.

Red Clover, Beebread, Cloveone, Cow Clover, Daidzein, Meadow Clover, Purple Clover, Wild Clover
Trifolium pratense

Red Clover flowers yield a yellow toned colorant used as a cosmetic or textile dye.

The mordant alum shades the tones toward gold.

Red Clover is a hardy perennial found in many regions of the world including Asia, Africa, Europe, North America, and South America. It is not particular regarding soil composition or nutrition and is sometimes cultivated to help fix nitrogen back into poor quality soils. Red Clover requires full sun and consistent moisture. It is easily propagated by seed and will self-sow readily if given its own place in the garden.

Red Poppy
Corn Poppy, Corn Rose, Flanders Poppy, Headwark, Red Weed
Papaver rhoeas

Red Poppy flowers yield a red toned colorant used as a culinary, cosmetic, or textile dye and sometimes used as an ink.

Red Poppy is a common wildflower adapted to many regions of the world including North America. Hardy to zone 5, it is not particular regarding soil composition but does prefer full sun and consistent moisture. Red Poppy can be propagated by seeds sown in the spring and will self-sow readily if given its own place in the garden.

Red Root, Sticky Laurel, Wild Snowball
Ceanothus velutinus

Red Root flowers yield a green colorant used as a culinary or textile dye.

Red root is a small shrub native to North America where it can be found growing in open glades & prairies. It is sometimes cultivated as an ornamental.

Red Root, Dye Root, Paint Root, Sprit Weed
Lachanthes caroliana

Red Root yields a red toned colorant used as a paint additive, textile dye, or cosmetic component.

Red Root is a perennial native to eastern North America. It prefers sandy or loamy soil, full or partial sun and consistent moisture.   It can be found growing wild in bogs and swamps. Red Root can be propagated by seed sown out in the spring or by spring division.

Redroot Pigweed
Amaranthus retroflexus

Redroot Pigweed yields a colorant in tones ranging from yellow to green depending on the age of the plant.

Redroot seed heads yield a red colorant used as a cosmetic or textile dye.

Redroot Pigweed is native to Central and South America and has been cultivated in other regions. Hardy to zone 5, it is not particular regarding soil composition but does prefer full sun and consistent moisture. Redroot Pigweed can be propagated by seed sown out in the spring and will self sow readily if given its own place in the garden.

Reed Mace, Cattail, Reedmace
Typha latifolia

Reedmace heads yield a colorant in shades ranging from red to brown depending on the age of the plant.

Reedmace is a perennial plant native to Africa, Europe, North America, and South America.

Rose, Cabbage Rose, Rose, Province Rose
Rosa sp.

Rose petals activated with lemon juice yield a pink toned colorant and the hips yield a yellow toned colorant used as a cosmetic, culinary, or textile dye.

Roses are cultivated as an aromatic ornamental in most regions of the world. They are not particular regarding soil composition but do prefer full to partial sun and consistent moisture. Roses are propagated by seed, cuttings taken in mid summer with a heel of the previous year's growth, division of suckers taken in the early spring or air layering.

Rosemary, Old Man, Romarin, Romero, Rusmari, Rusmary
Rosmarinus officinalis

Rosemary leaves and flowers yield a yellow toned colorant used in culinary, cosmetic and textile dyeing.

Rosemary is an evergreen shrub or herb native to Asia but has been naturalized in much of the world as a garden shrub and a kitchen herb. Hardy to zone 6, it prefers sandy to loamy soil, full sun, and consistent moisture.

Rose of Sharon
Hibiscus syriacus

The flowers of the Rose of Sharon yield a colorant that varies depending on the species. The most popular is the blue extracted from the blue spectrum flowers. The colorant is used as a culinary, cosmetic, or textile dye.

Rose of Sharon is spread throughout the world as both a cultivated ornamental and a wild growing mountain plant. It is easily propagated by seeds or softwood cuttings.

Rowan, Mountain Ash, Quickbeam, Sort Apple, Witchen
Sorbus aucuparia

The whole Rowan plant yields a black colorant used as a cosmetic, culinary and textile dye.

Rowan is native to Europe but the trees are cultivated as an ornamental in many areas. Hardy to zone 2, it is not particular regarding soil composition but does prefer full to partial sun and consistent moisture. Rowan can be propagated by seeds sown as soon as they are ripe.

Safflower, Alazor, American Saffron, Bastard Saffron, Benibana, Dyer's Saffron, Zaffer, Zafran
Carthamus tinctorius

Safflower flowers yield a commonly used dye product. It yields two colorants, the yellow and the red. The red ranges between shades of rose and scarlet and is the original colorant for rouge. The yellow provides shades within the golden tone range. The colorant tone is dependent on the flowers used when creating the dye bath.

Safflower is native to India, Africa, Europe, and North America but is cultivated elsewhere. It prefers sandy to loamy soils, full sun, and moist conditions. Safflower is easily propagated by seeds sown out in the spring.

Saffron, Azafron, Indian Saffron, Kashmira, Kesar, Kumkuma, Zafran
Crocus sativus

The stigmas of the Saffron yield a yellow toned colorant used as a culinary, cosmetic, and textile dye. Mordant – Alum.

Saffron petals yield a blue green toned colorant used as a cosmetic, culinary, or textile dye.

Saffron is native to India and the Mediterranean and cultivated elsewhere for use as a culinary seasoning. It is easily propagated by seeds sown in the spring.

Sage, Dalmatian Sage, Garden Sage, Meadow Sage, Sauge, Scarlet Sage, Spanish Sage, True Sage
Salvia officinalis

The sage plant yields a gray toned colorant used as a cosmetic, culinary, or textile dye.

Sage is native to the Mediterranean but has naturalized to Europe and is cultivated in North America. Hardy to zone 5, it prefers sandy or loamy soil, full sun, and consistent moisture. Sage can be propagated by seed sown out in the spring, cuttings taken at any time during the growing season or by spring layering.

Sage – Russian
Perovskia atriplicifolia

The flowers of Russian Sage yield a blue toned colorant used as a cosmetic, culinary or textile dye.

Sage Brush
Artemisia tridentate

Sage Brush leaves, buds, and stems yield a yellow to golden colorant used as a culinary, cosmetic, and textile dye.

Sage Brush is an evergreen shrub native to Central America & North America and cultivated in other regions. Hardy to zone 7, it prefers sandy to loamy soil, consistent moisture and requires full sun. Sage Bush can be propagated by seeds sown in the spring or cuttings taken in mid summer.

Gray Sage Bush, Chamiso, Chamiza, Fourwing Saltbush
Atriplex canescens

The leaves and stems of the Gray Sage Bush yield a yellow toned colorant used as a culinary, cosmetic, or textile dye.

Gray Sage Bush is native to Central America and the southwestern portion of North America. Hardy to zone 7, it prefers sandy to loamy soil, consistent moisture and requires full sun. Grey Sage Bush can be propagated by seeds sown in the spring or cuttings taken in mid summer.

Sapphireberry, Asiactic Sweetleaf
Symplocos paniculata

The bark and leaves of the Sapphireberry yield a red toned colorant used as a textile dye. Mordant – Alum.

Sapphireberry is a deciduous shrub native to Asia and cultivated in other regions.

Sassafras, Ague Tree, Cinnamon Wood, Root Bear Tree, Sassafras albidum

Sassafras bark and wood yield a brown toned colorant that tends toward yellow or orange depending on the mordant.

The leaves alone yield a yellow colorant used as a cosmetic, culinary, or textile dye.

Sassafras is native to the eastern coast of North America and is generally found growing on hilltops and ridges in mountainous areas. Hardy to zone 5, it is not particular regarding soil composition but does prefer full to partial sunlight and consistent moisture. It is propagated by seeds sown as soon as they are ripe, by root cuttings taken in the late winter or by division of the suckers in the early spring.

Sea Buckthorn, Argasse, Argousier, Chharma, Dhar Bu, Finbar, Grisset, Meerdorn, Oblepikha, Purging Thorn, Saddorn, Seedom, Star Bu, Tindved, Yellow Spine Hippophae rhamnoides

The young leaves and shoots of the Sea Buckthorn plant yield a black toned colorant and the fruit yields a yellow colorant used as a cosmetic, culinary, or textile dye.

Sea Buckthorn is a hardy shrub native to China and Russia but can also be found in other habitats and regions. It can be found growing wild along shorelines. Hardy to zone 3, it is not particular regarding soil composition but does prefer full sun and moist to wet conditions. It can be propagated by seed but is more often propagated by division of the suckers. It will self-propagate by runner and suckering if left alone.

Shallot, Gandana, Kanda

Allium ascalonicum

Shallot bulb skins yield a yellow toned colorant used as a cosmetic, culinary, or textile dye.

Shallot is a commonly cultivated food product whose native habitat is unknown. Hardy to zone 5, it prefers sandy or loamy soil, full sun and consistent moisture. Shallot is a bulb growing plant easily propagated by division of the bulbs.

Siberian Pine
Pinus pumila

Siberian Pine needles yield a tan to green toned colorant used as a textile dye.

Siberian Pine is a low growing evergreen tree native to mountainous regions. It can be propagated by seeds or semi-softwood cuttings.

Silk Tree, Mimosa
Albizia julibrissin

Silk Tree flower heads yield a yellow toned colorant used as a cosmetic, culinary, or textile dye.

Silk Tree is a deciduous tree native to Asia but cultivated in other frost-free regions. Hardy to zone 7, it is not particular regarding soil composition but does prefer full sun and dry to moist soil. Silk Tree can be propagated by seed soaked in water and then sown in the early spring, cuttings of new growth taken in the late summer, root cuttings taken in the winter or division of the suckers during the growing season.

Smoke Bush, Purple Smoke Bush, Smoke Tree
Cotinus coggygria

Smoke Bush roots and stems yield a yellowish-orange colorant used as a textile dye.

Smoke Bush is a deciduous shrub native to Asia and Europe and cultivated in other regions including North America.

Sorrel, Acedera, Azeda Brava, Common Sorrel, Field Sorrel, Garden, Sorrel Dock, Sour Dock
Rumex acetosa

Sorrel roots yield colorants ranging from dark green to dark grey or brown depending on the age of the plant. It is a self-mordanting textile dye.

Sorrel leaves and stem yield a grayish blue colorant used as a cosmetic, culinary, or textile dye.

Sorrel is native to Europe and has been cultivated in other areas.

Sheep's Sorrel, Red Sorrel, Sour Weed
Rumex acetosella

Sheep's Sorrel roots yield a dark green to dark grey colorant that does not require a mordant.

Sheep's Sorrel is a member of the sorrel family native to Asia and Europe but naturalized too many other countries including North America.

Skunk Bush
Rhus trilobata

Skunk Bush leaves yield a black to dark brown colorant with the fruits acting as a mordant.

Skunk Bush twigs yield a yellow toned textile dye and the fruit yields a pink washed tan self-mordanting colorant.

Skunk Bush is native to the southwestern parts of North America.

Sour Cherry, Albulak, Alubalu, Pie Cherry
Prunus cerasus

Sour Cherry fruits yield a green toned colorant used in culinary, cosmetic and textile dyeing.

Sour Cherry is a species of cherry native to Asia and Europe and naturalized to the United States where it is cultivated as an ornamental or for the fruits. Hardy to zone 3, it is not particular regarding soil composition but does prefer full to partial sun and consistent moisture. It can be propagated by seed, cuttings taken in mid-summer or by layering in the spring. Suckers can be divided during the dormant season.

Southernwood
Artemisia abrotanum

Southernwood branches yield a yellow colorant used as a cosmetic, culinary or textile dye.

Southernwood is native to Europe and naturalized to the United States. Hardy to zone 4, it is not particular regarding soil composition but does prefer full to partial sun and dry to moist conditions. Southernwood can be propagated by seeds sown out in the spring or cuttings taken in mid summer.

Speckled Alder, Grey Alder
Alnus rugosa

Speckled Alder bark yields a red to brown toned colorant used as a textile dye.

Speckled Alder is native to eastern North America. Hardy to zone 2, it is not particular regarding soil composition and will tolerate heavy, poor quality soil and has been used to fix nitrogen back into the soil. It does prefer full to partial sun and consistently moist to wet conditions. Speckled Alder can be propagated by seeds sown out as soon as they are ripe or cuttings taken in the late fall after the leaves have dropped from the branches.

St. John's Wort, Amber, Goatweed, Tipton Weed
Hypericum perforatum

St. John's Wort flowering tops yield a yellowish brown colorant and the whole plant yields a red colorant when infused in alcohol.

St. John's Wort dyes are used as textile and cosmetic dyes.

St. John's Wort is native to Africa, Asia, and Europe and is cultivated in other regions for supplemental purposes. Hardy to zone 3, it is not particular regarding soil composition but does prefer good drainage, full to partial sun and consistent moisture. It can be propagated by seeds sown out as soon as they are ripe or by division in the spring.

Sumac, Lemon Sumac
Rhus sp.

Lemon Sumac fruits yield a black colorant used as an ink or textile dye.

Other sumac fruits yield a lighter color tending toward red.

The inner bark yields a bright yellow colorant used as a textile dye.

Sumac leaves yield a tan toned colorant used as a textile dye.

Sumac is native to eastern North America. Hardy to zone 5, it is not particular regarding soil composition but does prefer full sun and dry to moist conditions. It can be propagated by seeds sown out as soon as they are ripe, cuttings taken in mid-summer, or divisions of the suckers in the winter.

Sunflower, Adityabhakt, Corono Solis, Marigold of Peru,
Helianthus annuus

The flower heads of the sunflower yield colorants ranging in tone from yellow to green used as a cosmetic, culinary, or textile dye. Mordant - Alum

Sunflower petals are used as a natural colorant in cosmetics, textile dyes, and other products to obtain a yellow or orange glow.

Sunflower is native to North America and is cultivated worldwide. Hardy to zone 7, it is not particular regarding soil composition but does prefer full or partial sunlight and dry to moist conditions. Sunflower is easily grown from seeds sown out in the spring.

Sweet Cherry, Bird Cherry, Cereza, Cherry, Gean, Wild Cherry
Prunus avium

Sweet Cherry leaves yield a green toned colorant and the fruits yield a grey tone used as a cosmetic, culinary or textile dye.

Sweet Cherry is native to Africa, Asia and Europe and has been naturalized to parts of North America. Hardy to zone 3, it is not particular regarding soil composition but does prefer full to partial sun and consistent moisture. Sweet Cherry can be propagated by seeds cold stored during the winter and sown in the spring, cuttings taken in mid summer, division of the suckers or layering.

Sweet Chestnut, Spanish Chestnut
Castanea sativa

Sweet Chestnut seed has been ground fine and used as a bleaching agent for cloth.

Sweet Chestnut is native to much of Europe and has been naturalized to other parts of the world including the United States. Hardy to zone 5, it is not particular regarding soil composition but does prefer full sun and dry to moist conditions. Sweet Chestnut can be propagated by seeds sown as soon as it is ripe in a location protected from foraging creatures.

Tansy, Bitter Buttons, Hind Heal, Parsley Fern, Scented Fern, Stinking Willie
Tanacetum vulgare

The flowering tops of the tansy yield a yellow colorant used as a textile dye.

Tansy stalks and flower mixed yield tones ranging from gold to olive green. The higher the stalk content, the greener the tone. Mordant – Alum.

Tansy is native to Asia and Europe but has been naturalized to other regions including the United States where it can be found in cultivated gardens and growing wild along roadsides and untended areas.

Tea, Black Tea, Chinese Tea, English Tea, Green Tea, Tea
Camellia sinensis

Tea flower petals yield a greenish gray to black toned colorant used as a textile dye.

Tea leaves yield a tan to deep brown toned colorant used as a cosmetic, culinary, or textile dye.

Tea is cultivated in many parts of the world as a commonly consumed beverage. Hardy to zone 8, it prefers sandy to loamy soils with good drainage, partial sun, and consistent moisture. Tea can be propagated by seeds sown out as soon as they are ripe or by cuttings taken at any time during the growing season.

Black, brown, and green teas come from the same plant and the difference in coloring is a result of a change in the way that the tea is handled during processing. The more extensive the handling, the darker the tea product and resulting colorant. Brown Tea is only partially fermented while Black Tea is fully fermented and Green Tea is not fermented.

Teasel, Barber's Brush, Brushes & Combs, Card Thistle, Church Broom, Fuller's Teazel
Dipsacus sativus

Teasel yields a blue toned colorant used as an indigo alternative and a yellow toned colorant when alum mordant is used.

Teasel grows wild in parts of Africa, Asia, Europe and North America. It is not particular regarding soil composition but does prefer full sun and consistent moisture. It is easily propagated by seed and will self-sow readily.

Thimbleberry, Salmonberry

Rubus spectabilis

Thimbleberry fruits yield a purple to blue colorant used as a culinary, cosmetic, or textile dye.

Thimbleberry is native to Central America and North America where they are cultivated as a fragrant ornamental.

Tormentil, Septfoil, Tormentilla
Potentilla erecta

Tormentil root yields a self-mordanting red colorant used as a textile dye.

Tormentil is an herbaceous perennial native to Asia and Europe and naturalized to other areas including North America.   Hardy to zone 5, it is not particular regarding soil composition but does prefer full to partial shade and consistent moisture. Tormentil can be propagated by seeds sown in the spring or division.

Tree of Heaven, Ailante, Ailanto, Chinese Sumach, Copal Tree, Heaven Tree, Indian Tree of Heaven, Paradise Tree
Ailanthus altissima

Tree of Heaven leaves yield a yellow toned colorant used as a textile dye.

Tree of Heaven is native to the northeast and central Asia and has been naturalized to Europe and the United States. Hardy to zone 7, it prefers sandy or loamy soil, full to partial sun and moist to wet conditions. Tree of Heaven can be propagated by seeds sown out as soon as they are ripe, division of the suckers in the spring or root cuttings taken in mid-winter.

Tulip Tree, Canoe Tree, White Wood, Yellow Wood
Liriodendron tulipfera

Tulip Tree bark yields a gold toned colorant used as a textile dye.

Tulip Tree is native to eastern North America and cultivated elsewhere as an ornamental. Hardy to zone 4, it is not particular regarding soil composition but does prefer full sun, high nutrition, and consistent moisture.

Tulip Tree can be propagated by seeds sown out as soon as they are ripe or more successfully by layering in the spring.

Turmeric, Curcuma, Halada, Haldi, Haridra, Indian Saffron, Nisha, Rajani, Yu Jin
Curcuma longa, Curcuma zedoaria

Turmeric yields a bright yellow colorant used as a cosmetic, culinary and textile dye.

Turmeric is a shrub native to India and cultivated in China. It requires warm temperatures and heavy moisture to survive.

Uva Ursi, Arberry, Bearberry, Bearsgrape, Manzanita, Mountain Box, Mountain Cranberry, Ptarmigan Berry, Redberry, Rockberry, Sadberry
Arctostaphylos uva-ursi

Uva Ursi leaves yield a self-mordanting yellow to brown toned colorant used as a textile dye.

Uva Ursi fruits yield a grayish brown toned colorant used as a cosmetic or textile dye.

Uva Ursi is native to Asia, Europe, and North America. Hardy to zone 4, it prefers sandy or loamy soil, full to partial sun and consistent moisture. Uva Ursi can be propagated by seeds sown out as soon as they are ripe, cuttings taken in the late spring or division in the early spring.

Walnut, Akschota, English Walnut, He Tao, Juglands, Juglandis, Nogal, Walnussblatter
Juglans regia

Walnut hulls yield a dark brownish-black colorant used to dye fabrics, as hair colorant, or as part of sunless tanning lotions.

Walnut roots & bark yield a colorant ranging from dark purple to black used as a textile dye.

Unripe Walnut husks yield a yellow toned colorant and the catkins yield a bronzed brown tone when taken early in the season.

Walnut is the seed of the trees in the Jugulans family. There are numerous types of Walnut trees commonly used, with the Black Walnut being the most commonly cultivated. Walnut trees are tolerant of a wide range of soil composition but they do prefer full sun and consistent moisture. Walnut can be propagated by seeds sown out as soon as they are ripe and some varieties can be propagated by cuttings taken from new growth in the early spring.

Weld, Dyer's Weed
Reseda luteola

Weld flowers produce a bright yellow colorant and is the most lightfast of all yellow dyes.

The flower and stalk of the weld plant yield a true yellow textile dye. Mordant – Alum

The flower and stalk of the weld plant can be toned to yield a greenish yellow dye. Mordant – Copper

Weld is biennial growing 2-4 feet in height and native to Asia, Turkey, and Europe and naturalized to North America. Weld has been used as a dye since ancient times.

White Mulberry, Chi Sang, Mulberry, Mon Tea, Mora, Silkworm Mulberry
Morus alba

White Mulberry wood yields a brown colorant used as a cosmetic, culinary and textile dye.

White Mulberry is native to China where it is traditionally used as a food source for silkworms. White Mulberry has been naturalized to the United States.

Willow, Beak Willow (Salix bebbiana), Black Willow (Salix nigra), Coyote Willow (Salix exigua), Purple Willow (Salix purpurea), White Willow (Salix alba)
Salix sp.

Willow root and bark yield a black colorant with red undertones used as a textile dye.

Willow root alone yields a peachier red tone.

Willow trees are primarily found in Central America, Europe, and North America though they are cultivated in other areas.

Winterberry, Black Alder, Canada Holly, Fever Bush
Ilex verticillata

Winterberry roots yield a colorant in tones of red to orange depending on the age of the bush. The colorants are used cosmetics and textile dyeing.

Winterberry is a type of holly native to North America where it is cultivated as an ornamental.

Woad, Ben Lan Gen, Chinese Indigo, Dyer's Woad, Farberwaid, Glastum, Hierba Pastel, Indigo Woad, Isatis, Quing Dai
Isatis tinctoria

Woad leaves yield a colorant that creates shades of blue slightly less rich than indigo. Woad dye is processed in stages. The leaves are fermented, dried, re-fermented and then rinsed in lime water for the deepest dye product.

Woad is native to Asia but is naturalized to Europe and North America where it has been cultivated as a blue dye product for thousands of years.

Wood Betony
Stachys officinalis

Wood Betony leaves yield a yellow toned colorant used as a textile dye.

Wood betony is native to Europe but has been naturalized to many temperate regions of the world. Hardy to zone 7, it is not particular regarding soil composition but does prefer full or partial sun and consistent moisture. Betony is easy to grow from cuttings, root division, and seed.

Woodruff, Sweet Woodruff
Asperula odorata

Sweet Woodruff root yields a red toned colorant and the stems and leaves yield a greenish gray toned colorant used in textile dyeing.

The leaves of another species of Woodruff, Asperula tinctoria known as Dyer's Woodruff, yields a red toned colorant used as a cosmetic or textile dye. Mordant - Alum

Woodruff is native to Africa and Europe but is cultivated in other areas. Hardy to zone 5, it is not particular regarding soil composition, but does prefer full or partial shade and consistent moisture. Woodruff can be propagated by seeds sown out as soon as they are ripe, spring division, or by cuttings taken after flowering.

Woolly Manzanita, Downy Manzanita, Wollyleaf Manzantia
Arctostaphylos tomentosa

Woolly Manzanita leaves yield a self-mordanting yellow to brown toned colorant used as a culinary, cosmetic, or textile dye.

Woolly Manzanita is native to southwestern North America. Hardy to zone 8, it prefers sandy to loamy soil, full to partial sun and consistent moisture. Woolly Manzanita is propagated by seed sown out as soon as it is ripe, cuttings taken during the growing season or division in the early spring.

Yarrow, Achilee, Common Yarrow, Devil's Nettle, Milfoil, Nosebleed, Old Man's Pepper, Soldier's Woundwort, Staunchweed
Achillea millefolium

The flower and stalk of the yellow blooming yarrow yields a true yellow dye. Mordant – Alum.

Yarrow is native to Asia and Europe and has been naturalized to North America growing wild in dry fields and untended areas. Hardy to zone 2, it is not particular regarding soil composition but does prefer full or partial sunlight and dry to moist conditions. It can be propagated by seed but is more commonly propagated by spring division or cuttings. Seeds require full sunlight for germination.

Yellowroot
Xanthorhiza simplicissima

Yellowroot yields a yellow colorant used as a textile dye.

Yellowroot is native to the United States where it can be found growing wild along streams or cultivated as an ornamental groundcover.

Yellow Toadflax, Brideweed, Butter & Eggs, Buttered Hayhocks, Calves Snout, Churnstaff, Devil's Head, Devil's Ribbon, Doggies, Dragon Bushes, Eggs & Bacon, Eggs & Collops, Flaxweed, Gallwort, Larkspur, Lion's Mouth, Monkey Flower, Pennywort, Rabbits, Ramsted, Toadpipe, Wild Snapdraggon, Yellow Rod
Linaria vulgaris

Yellow Toadflax flowers yield a yellow toned colorant used as a cosmetic or textile dye.

Yellow Toadflax is native to Asia and Europe and has been naturalized to the United States where it is considered an invasive weed by some. It is easily propagated by seeds sown out in the spring.

Zinnia
Zinnia elegans

The flowers of the zinnia yield a colorant ranging in tones from beige to deep tan. Mordant – Alum

The zinnia is an easy to grow annual reaching heights of 1-3 feet and blooming red, orange, and pink flowers from spring to first frost.

Glossary of Terms

Acid – An acid produces a pH of less than 7 in water. Having a low pH.

Adjective - Adjective dyes are those dyes that require use of a mordant to bind the color to the fiber.

Alkali – An alkali produces a pH of more than 7. Having a high pH.

Alopecia – Baldness. The partial or complete loss of hair.

Alum (aluminum sulfate) - Alum is a naturally occurring basic mordant.

Alum (aluminum acetate) - A naturally occurring common mordant.

Aniline - Aniline dyes or basic dyes are a class of synthetic dyes derived from coal tar that produce brilliant colors but poor colorfastness.

Anti-Microbial- A substance that kills or inhibits the growth of microorganisms

Aromatic – A substance having a pleasant and distinctive smell that is used as a treatment.

Aroma Therapy – Aromatic plant extracts or essential oils to cause a physical or psychological effect in treatments.

Aspergillus - A type of common mold that cause food spoilage and potentially disease.

Bleeding – Color rinsing out of a dyed textile.

Botanical Name – The Latin name give to a species of plant to distinguish it from other plants.

Chrome – (Potassium Dichromate) Chrome is a naturally occurring common mordant.

Citric Acid – Acid found in many plant products but most common to citrus fruits. Citric Acid is used to neutralize high pH.

Colorant - Substance that colors something usually food, cosmetics, or textile products.

Colorfastness – A measure of how resistant a dye material is to fading.

Common Name – The non-specific name used for everyday reference to a plant

Comminution – The action of reducing a material or substance. When processing plants the act of reducing the size of the plant parts by cutting, grinding, or pounding

Copper (copper sulphate) – Copper is a naturally occurring mordant used to give green casts to textiles.

Copperas – Term used for iron ore (ferrous sulfate) used to depress the colors of a dye bath.

Cream of Tarter (potassium bitartrate) - A naturally occurring color modifier. Cream of Tarter is not a stand-alone mordant but acts in tandem with other mordants.

Decoction – The result of concentration the essence of a substance or plant part by heating or boiling.

Dram – A unit of measurement equaling approximately 1/16 of a dry weight ounce in US measurement 1/8 of a fluid ounce in Apothecary measurement.

Dye – Color-bearing organic compounds that penetrate fiber or other matter.

Dyebath – A solution of colorant and water used to color textiles.

Dyestuff – Any raw material that releases dye.

Expression - The process of forcibly separating liquids from solids.

Fluid extract – A type of fluid-solid substance obtained from plant matter through water or alcohol processing

Fugitive Color – Color that is prone to fading when exposed to sunlight or washing.

Hydration - The process of combining with or giving water.

Hypoallergenic – A substance unlikely to cause an allergic reaction.

Histamine - The chemical released by the body during an allergic reaction.

Infusion – Aqueous – A drink or extract made by soaking plant parts in water.

Infusion – Oil – A drink, extract, or product made by soaking plant parts in oil.

Iron Ore (ferrous sulfate) used to mute or darken the colors of a dye bath.

Lighfastness - A measure of a dye products resistance to fading from light exposure.

Lye (sodium hydroxide) – A caustic substance used to shift pH.

Maceration – Softening plant materials by soaking or steeping in a liquid. To separate the compounds by soaking or steeping

Mordant – A substance that combines with a dye or stain to fix the colorant into a material. A mordant may brighten, darken, or otherwise alter the tone of a color in fabric.

Natural Dye – Dye derived from animal, mineral, or plant matter.

Natural Fiber – A fiber obtained from an animal, mineral, or plant source.

Over Dye – The act of placing one dye over another to alter the finished tone.

Percolation - The extraction of soluble components by passing the liquid through a filtering medium.

pH – A scale for measuring the acidity or alkalinity of a substance. A pH of 7 is neutral. Low pH is acidic. High pH is alkaline.

Proof Spirit – A mixture of alcohol and water containing 50% alcohol by volume standard in the US.

Reactive Dye – A class of synthetic dyes that are used to dye natural fibers that traditionally resist taking color.

Rubefacient – A substance whose external application produces increased circulation or redness of the skin.

Saponins – A class of steroid and terpenoid glycosides that are used in detergents and foam when shaken with water.

Squalene – An oily liquid that is the precursor to sterols.

Sterols – Naturally occurring unsaturated steroid alcohols.

Substantive Dyes – Dyes that produce lasting color without the use of a mordant.

Tannin – A naturally occurring component of some plant products used as a mordant. It aids some dyes in being self-mordanting and shifts colors to a browner tone.

Tin (stannous chloride) - A metallic salt used as a brightening mordant.

Tincture – A substance made by dissolving plant materials in alcohol.

Viscosity – The resistance of a liquid to movement and flow.

Washfastness - A measure of how resistant a dye product is to fading over time due to exposure to water or soap.

References

Full reference list from a compendium of beneficial herbs and oils. Personal observations, experimentations, and family notes Laurie Pippen

A. Abdul Rahuman, Geetha Gopalakrishnan, P. Venkatesan and Kannappan Geetha (2008). "Isolation and identification of mosquito larvicidal compound from Abutilon indicum (Linn.) Sweet". Parasitology Research 102

A. Ngan & R. Conduit (2011). "A double-blind, placebo-controlled investigation of the effects of Passiflora incarnata (passionflower) herbal tea on subjective sleep quality". Phytotherapy Research 25

Abbott, I. A. (1996). Ethnobotany of seaweeds: clues to uses of seaweeds. Hydrobiologia.

Adhami, VM; Aziz, MH; Mukhtar, H; Ahmad, N (2003). "Activation of prodeath Bcl-2 family proteins and mitochondrial apoptosis pathway by sanguinarine in immortalized human HaCaT keratinocytes". Clinical cancer research 9

Agrawal, K. (1992). Biochemical pharmacology of blood and bloodforming organs. Berlin: Springer-Verlag.

Agarwal R, Gupta SK, Agrawal SS, Srivastava S, Saxena R (2008). "Oculohypotensive effects of foeniculum vulgare in experimental models of glaucoma". Indian J. Physiol. Pharmacol. 52

Ahmad, Nihal; Gupta, Sanjay; Husain, Mirza M.; Heiskanen, Kaisa M.; Mukhtar, Hasan (2000). "Differential Antiproliferative and Apoptotic Response of Sanguinarine for Cancer Cells versus Normal Cells". Clinical Cancer Research 6

Aiyer HS, Kichambare S, Gupta RC 2008. Prevention of oxidative DNA damage by bioactive berry components. Nutritional Cancer. 60

Ajai K. Chemical composition of the essential oil from fresh leaves of Melaleuca leucadendron L. from north India. Journal of Essential Oil-Bearing Plants. CABI Abstracts.

Akatsuka, I. (1990). Introduction to applied phycology. The Hague: SPB Academic Pub. bv.

Akihisa, Toshihiro; Higo, Naoki; Tokuda, Harukuni; Ukiya, Motohiko; Akazawa, Hiroyuki; Tochigi, Yuichi; Kimura, Yumiko; Suzuki, Takashi et al. (2007). "Cucurbitane-type triterpenoids from the fruits of Momordica charantia and their cancer chemopreventive effects". Journal of Natural Products 70

Allaby, M. (1998). A dictionary of plant sciences (2nd ed.). New York: Oxford University Press.

Allahverdiyev, A; Duran, N; Ozguven, M; Koltas, S (2004). "Antiviral activity of the volatile oils of L. Against virus type-2". Phytomedicine 11

Almajano, M. Pilar; Carbó, Rosa; Jiménez, J. Angel López; Gordon, Michael H. (2008). "Antioxidant and antimicrobial activities of tea infusions". Food Chemistry 108

Amer A. Repellency effect of forty-one essential oils against Aedes, American Chemical Society.Biology of Plants 2005

Anderson T, Foght J (2001). "Weight loss and delayed gastric emptying following a South American herbal preparation in overweight patients". J Hum Nutr Diet 14

Anopheles and Culex mosquitoes. Parasitol Res. 2006

American Journal of Botany. (n.d.). from http://www.amjbot.org

American Journal of Clinical Nutrition. (n.d.). Retrieved June 19, 2014, from http://ajcn.nutrition.org/content/by/year

Andrade, G; E Esteban, L Velasco, MJ Lorite, EJ Bedmar (1997). "Isolation and identification of N2-fixing microorganisms from the rhizosphere of Capparis spinosa (L.).". Plant and Soil (Kluwer Academic Publishers) 197

Angier, B. (1978). Field guide to medicinal wild plants. Harrisburg, Pa.: Stackpole Books.

"Antimicrobial activity of Calendula officinalis petal extracts against fungi, as well as Gram-negative and Gram-positive clinical pathogens". Complement Ther Clin Pract 18

Aphrodisiac activity of methanol extract of leaves of Passiflora incarnata Linn. in mice". Phytotherapy Research 17

Appa Rao MVR, Srinivas K, Koteshwar Rao T. "The effect of Mandookaparni (Centella asiatica) on the general mental ability (medhya) of mentally retarded children". J. Res Indian Med. 1973

Arrigoni-Blank Mde F , Oliveira RL , Mendes SS , et al. Seed germination, phenology, and antiedematogenic activity of Peperomia pellucida (L.) H. B. K. BMC Pharmacol . 2002

Aronson, J. (2009). Meyler's side effects of herbal medicines. Amsterdam: Elsevier. Auf'mkolk, M.; Ingbar, J. C.; Kubota, K.; Amir, S. M.; Ingbar, S. H. (1985). "Extracts and Auto-Oxidized Constituents of Certain Plants Inhibit the Receptor-Binding and the Biological Activity of Graves' Immunoglobulins". Endocrinology 116

Austin, DF (2004). Florida Ethnobotany. Boca Raton, FL: CRC Press.

Australian journal of herbal medicine. (n.d.). Concord West, N.S.W.: National Herbalists Association of Australia.

Avadhani, Mythili et al.; The Sweetness and Bitterness of Sweet Flag [Acorus calamus L.] – A Review; Research Journal of Pharmaceutical, Biological and Chemical Sciences, Volume 4, Issue 2

Awad, Rosalie; Muhammad, Asim; Durst, Tony; Trudeau, Vance L.; Arnason, John T. (2009). "Bioassay-guided fractionation of lemon balm (Melissa officinalisL.) using anin vitromeasure of GABA transaminase activity". Phytotherapy Research 23

Aziba PI , Adedeji A , Ekor M , Adeyemi O (2001). "Analgesic activity of Peperomia pellucida aerial parts in mice". Fitoterapia 72

Babykutty, S.; Padikkala, J.; Sathiadevan, P. P.; Vijayakurup, V.; Azis, T. K.; Srinivas, P.; Gopala, S. (2008). "Apoptosis induction of Centella asiatica on human breast cancer cells". African journal of traditional, complementary, and alternative medicines : AJTCAM / African Networks on Ethnomedicines 6

Badar, VA; Thawani, VR; Wakode, PT; Shrivastava, MP; Gharpure, KJ; Hingorani, LL; Khiyani, RM (2005). "Efficacy of Tinospora cordifolia in allergic rhinitis". Journal of Ethnopharmacology 96

Bailey DG, Dresser GK (2004). "Interactions between grapefruit juice and cardiovascular drugs". Am J Cardiovasc Drugs

Bailey, L.H.; Bailey, E.Z.; the staff of the Liberty Hyde Bailey Hortorium. 1976. Hortus third: A concise dictionary of plants cultivated in the United States and Canada. Macmillan, New York.

Balakumbahan, R.; K. Rajamani and K. Kumanan (29 December 2010). Acorus calamus. Journal of Medicinal Plants Research 4 (25): 2740–2745. Retrieved 14 May 2011.

Barnard, Edward S. & Yates, Sharon Fass, ed. (1998). "Trees". Reader's Digest North American Wildlife: Trees and Nonflowering Plants. The Reader's Digest Association, Inc.

Barnes, J., & Anderson, L. (2002). Herbal medicines: A guide for healthcare professionals. (2nd ed.). London: Pharmaceutical Press.

Bakshi N., Kumar P., Sharma M. "Antidermatophytic activity of some alkaloids from Solanum dulcamara." Indian Drugs. 45

Barton, DL; Soori, GS; Bauer, BA; Sloan, JA; Johnson, PA; Figueras, C; Duane, S; Mattar, B et al. (2010). "Pilot study of Panax quinquefolius (American ginseng) to improve cancer-related fatigue: a randomized, double-blind, dose-finding evaluation: NCCTG trial N03CA.". Supportive care in cancer : official journal of the Multinational Association of Supportive Care in Cancer 18

Bastos JF. Moreira IJ. Ribeiro TP. Medeiros IA. Antoniolli AR. De Sousa DP. Santos MR. Hypotensive and vasorelaxant effects of citronellol, a monoterpene alcohol, in rats. Basic & Clinical Pharmacology & Toxicology. 106. 2010

Bayma JD , Arruda MS , Müller AH , Arruda AC , Canto WC . A dimeric ArC 2 compound from Peperomia pellucida . Phytochemistry . 2000

Beal, J. (1981). Natural products as medicinal agents: Plenary lectures of the International Research Congress on Medicinal Plant Research, Strasbourg, July 1980. Stuttgart: Hippokrates Verlag.

Bean, W. J. (1970). Trees and Shrubs Hardy in the British Isles. John Murray, London.

Beloin, N.; Gbeassor, M.; Akpagana, K.; Hudson, J.; De Soussa, K.; Koumaglo, K.; Arnason, J. T. (2005). "Ethnomedicinal uses of Momordica charantia (Cucurbitaceae) in Togo and relation to its phytochemistry and biological activity". Journal of Ethnopharmacology 96

Benedek B., Geisz N., Jäger W., Thalhammer T., Kopp B. Choleretic effects of yarrow (Achillea millefolium s.l.) in the isolated perfused rat liver. Phytomedicine 2006

Benedek, Birgit; Kopp, Brigitte (2007). "Achillea millefolium L. S.I. Revisited: Recent findings confirm the traditional use". Wiener Medizinische Wochenschrift 157

Bensky. Clavey. Stoger. (2004). Gamble Chinese Herbal Medicine

Bensky, Dan; Andrew Gamble, Steven Clavey, Erich Stöger (2004). Chinese Herbal Medicine: Materia Medica, 3rd Edition. Eastland Press.

Bent S, Kane C, Shinohara K, et al (February 2006). "Saw palmetto for benign prostatic hyperplasia". N. Engl. J. Med. 354

Blevi, V., & Sween, G. (1993). Aromatherapy. New York: Avon Books.

Balchin, M. (2006). Aromatherapy Science: A guide for healthcare professionals. London [u.a.: Pharmaceutical Press.

Bhatnagar M. Sisodia SS. Antisecretory and antiulcer activity of Asparagus racemosus Willd. against indomethacin plus phyloric ligation-induced gastric ulcer in rats. Journal of Herbal Pharmacotherapy. 6

Bialonska D, Kasimsetty SG, Khan SI, Ferreira D (11 November 2009). "Urolithins, intestinal microbial metabolites of Pomegranate ellagitannins, exhibit potent antioxidant activity in a cell-based assay". J Agric Food Chem 57

Bilušić Vundać V., Brantner A.H., Plazibat M. "Content of polyphenolic constituents and antioxidant activity of some Stachys taxa" Food Chemistry 2007 104

Blamey, M. & Grey-Wilson, C. (1989). Flora of Britain and Northern Europe. Hodder & Stoughton.

Blanco MM, Costa CA, Freire AO, Santos JG, Costa M (March 2009). "Neurobehavioral effect of essential oil of Cymbopogon citratus in mice". Phytomedicine

Bloomfield, H. (1998). Healing anxiety with herbs. New York, NY: HarperCollins.

Blumenthal, M. (2000). Herbal medicine: Expanded Commission E monographs ; herb monographs, based on those created by a Special Expert Committee of the German Federal Institute for Drugs and Medical Devices (1.st ed.). Newton, Mass.: Integrative Medicine Communications.

Boaz M, Leibovitz E, Bar Dayan Y, Wainstein J (2011). "Functional foods in the treatment of type 2 diabetes: olive leaf extract, turmeric and fenugreek, a qualitative review". Func Foods Health Dis 1

Bojo AC , Albano-Garcia E , Pocsidio GN (1994). "The antibacterial activity of Peperomia pellucida (L.) HBK (Piperaceae)". Asia Life Sci 3: 35–44.

^ Ragasa CY , Dumato M , Rideout JA (1998). "Antifungal compounds from Peperomia pellucida". ACGC Chem Res Commun 7

Bopana N. Saxena S. Asparagus racemosus--ethnopharmacological evaluation and conservation needs. [Review] [77 refs] Journal of Ethnopharmacology. 110

Böttger, Stefan; Melzig, Matthias F. (2011). "Triterpenoid saponins of the Caryophyllaceae and Illecebraceae family". Phytochemistry Letters 4

Boyer, Jeanelle; Liu, RH; Rui Hai Liu (May 2004). "Apple phytochemicals and their health benefits". Nutrition journal Cornell University, Ithaca, New York 14853-7201 USA: Department of Food Science and Institute of Comparative and Environmental Toxicology 3

Boyle, P; Robertson C, Lowe F, Roehrborn C (Apr 2004). "Updated meta-analysis of clinical trials of Serenoa repens extract in the treatment of symptomatic benign prostatic hyperplasia". BJU Int 93

Bradley (1992). British Herbal Compendium 1. Bournemouth, England: British Herbal Medicine Association.

Bradwejn, J.; Zhou, Y.; Koszycki, D.; Shlik, J. (2000). "A double-blind, placebo-controlled study on the effects of Gotu Kola (Centella asiatica) on acoustic startle response in healthy subjects". Journal of clinical psychopharmacology 20

Bramati, Lorenzo; Minoggio, Markus; Gardana, Claudio; Simonetti, Paolo; Mauri, Pierluigi; Pietta, Piergiorgio (2002). "Quantitative Characterization of Flavonoid Compounds in Rooibos Tea (Aspalathus linearis) by LC−UV/DAD". Journal of Agricultural and Food Chemistry 50

Braun, L., & Cohen, M. (2006). Herbs and Natural Supplements Inkling an Evidence-Based Guide. London: Elsevier Health Sciences APAC.

Bremness, L. (1988). The complete book of herbs. New York: Viking Studio Books.

Bressler R (2006). "Grapefruit juice and drug interactions. Exploring mechanisms of this interaction and potential toxicity for certain drugs". Geriatrics 61

Brickell, C. (1994). The Royal Horticultural Society gardeners' encyclopedia of plants and flowers (Rev. ed.). London: Dorling Kindersley.

Brinkhause, B., Lindner, M., et al., "Chemical, Pharmacological and Clinical Profile of The East Asian Medical Plant 2000

British pharmacopoeia 1975. (1975). London: H.M.S.O.

British pharmacopoeia 2013. (2013). London: H.M.S.O.

Brown, D. (1996). Aromatherapy. Lincolnwood, Ill.: NTC Pub.

Brunke, E. (1986). Progress in essential oil research: Proceedings of the International Symposium on Essential Oils, Holzminden/Neuhaus, Federal Republic of Germany, September 18-21, 1985. Berlin: W. de Gruyter.

Bui LT, Nguyen DT, Ambrose PJ (2006). "Blood pressure and heart rate effects following a single dose of bitter orange". The Annals of Pharmacotherapy 40

Burdette JE, Liu J, Chen SN, Fabricant DS, Piersen CE, Barker EL, Pezzuto JM, Mesecar A, Van Breemen RB, Farnsworth NR, Bolton JL (2003). "Black cohosh acts as a mixed competitive ligand and partial agonist of the serotonin receptor". J. Agric. Food Chem. 51

Burk D.R., Cichacz Z.A., Daskalova S.M. Aqueous extract of Achillea millefolium L. (Asteraceae) inflorescences suppresses lipopolysaccharide-induced inflammatory responses in RAW 264.7 murine macrophages. Journal of Medicinal Plant Research 2010

Caceres, A. "Plants used in Guatemala for the treatment of gastrointestinal disorders. 1. Screening of 84 plants against enterobacteria." J. Ethnopharmacol. 1990

Canning S, Waterman M, Orsi N, Ayres J, Simpson N, Dye L (March 2010). "The efficacy of Hypericum perforatum (St John's wort) for the treatment of premenstrual syndrome: a randomized, double-blind, placebo-controlled trial". CNS Drugs 24

Carson, C. F.; Hammer, K. A.; Riley, T. V. (2006). "Melaleuca alternifolia (Tea Tree) Oil: a Review of Antimicrobial and Other Medicinal Properties". Clinical Microbiology Reviews 19

Cassileth, B. (1998). The alternative medicine handbook: The complete reference guide to alternative and complementary therapies. New York: W.W. Norton.

Castleman, M., & Hendler, S. (1991). The healing herbs: The ultimate guide to the curative power of nature's medicines. Emmaus, Pa.: Rodale Press.

Castner, J., & Timme, S. (1998). A field guide to medicinal and useful plants of the Upper Amazon. Gainesville, FL: Feline Press.

Castro, M. (1991). The complete homeopathy handbook: A guide to everyday health care. New York: St. Martin's Press.

Cataldo, A., Gasbarro, V., et al., "Effectiveness of the Combination of Alpha Tocopherol, Rutin, Melilotus, and Centella asiatica in The Treatment of Patients With Chronic Venous Insufficiency", Minerva Cardioangiology, 2001

Ceccarelli N., Curadi M., Picciarelli P., Martelloni L., Sbrana C., Giovannetti M. "Globe artichoke as a functional food" Mediterranean Journal of Nutrition and Metabolism 2010

Cecchini C, Cresci A, Coman MM, et al. (June 2007). "Antimicrobial activity of seven hypericum entities from central Italy". Planta Med. 73

Cerda JJ, Robbins FL, Burgin CW, Baumgartner TG, Rice RW (September 1988). "The effects of grapefruit pectin on patients at risk for coronary heart disease without altering diet or lifestyle". Clin Cardiol 11

Chaiyana W., Okonogi S."Inhibition of cholinesterase by essential oil from food plant". Phytomedicine. 2012.

Chan A, Graves V, Shea TB, A For prevention of dementia: (2006). Journal of Alzheimer's Disease 9

Chan E (1993). "Displacement of bilirubin from albumin by berberine". Biology of the Neonate 63

Chan, E.W.C. et al. (2009). "Effects of different drying methods on the antioxidant properties of leaves and tea of ginger species". Food Chemistry 113

Chan Y.-S., Cheng L.-N., Wu J.-H., Chan E., Kwan Y.-W., Lee S.M.-Y., Leung G.P.-H., Yu P.H.-F., Chan S.-W.,"A review of the pharmacological effects of Arctium lappa (burdock)" [Article in Press] Inflammopharmacology 2010

Chen, G, Sun, W-B, & Sun, H. (2007). Ploidy variation in Buddleja L. (Buddlejaceae) in the Sino - Himalayan region and its biogeographical implications. Botanical Journal of the Linnean Society. 2007

Chen R., Liu Z., Zhao J., Chen R., Meng F., Zhang M., Ge W. "Antioxidant and immunobiological activity of water-soluble polysaccharide fractions purified from Acanthopanax senticosu" Food Chemistry 2011

Chevallier, A. (1996). The encyclopedia of medicinal plants. New York: DK Pub.

Chevallier, A. (2000). Natural health encyclopedia of herbal medicine (2nd American ed.). New York: DK Pub.

Cheung SC, Szeto YT, Benzie IF (March 2007). "Antioxidant protection of edible oils". Plant Foods Hum Nutr 62

Chiang, Y. M.; Lo, C. P.; Chen, Y. P.; Wang, S. Y.; Yang, N. S.; Kuo, Y. H.; Shyur, L. F. (2005). "Ethyl caffeate suppresses NF-κB activation and its downstream inflammatory mediators, iNOS, COX-2, and PGE2in vitroor in mouse skin". British Journal of Pharmacology 146

Chidrawar, VR; Patel, KN; Sheth, NR; Shiromwar, SS; Trivedi, P (2011). "Antiobesity effect of Stellaria media against drug induced obesity in Swiss albino mice". Ayu 32

Chiej, R. (1984). The Macdonald encyclopedia of medicinal plants. London: Macdonald.

Chinese Materia Medica (1998). Beijing University of Traditional Chinese Medicine

Chittenden, F. (1951) RHS Dictionary of Plants plus Supplement. Oxford University Press.

Chopra, R. (1956). Glossary of Indian medicinal plants,. New Delhi: Council of Scientific & Industrial Research.

Chopra, R., & Chopra, R. (1969). Supplement to glossary of Indian medicinal plants. New Delhi: Publications and Information Directorate.

Chopra, R. (1992). Second supplement to Glossary of Indian medicinal plants with active principles. New Delhi: Publications & Information Directorate, CSIR.

135

Chopra, R. N.; Nayar, S. L.; Chopra, I. C. Glossary of Indian Medicinal Plants. 1986. New Delhi: Council of Scientific and Industrial Research.

Choudhary M.I., Jalil S., Todorova M., Trendafilova A., Mikhova B., Duddeck H. Inhibitory effect of lactone fractions and individual components from three species of the Achillea millefolium complex of Bulgarian origin on the human neutrophils respiratory burst activity. Natural Product Research 2007

Chui C.H., Gambari R., Lau F.Y., Teo I.T.N., Ho K.P., Cheng G.Y.M., Ke B., Higa T., Kok H.L., Chan A.S.C., Tang J.C.O."Anti-cancer potential of traditional Chinese herbal medicines and microbial fermentation products." Minerva Biotecnologica. 17. 2005.

Clarke, D. L. (1988). W. J. Bean Trees and Shrubs Hardy in the British Isles, Supplement. John Murray

Clement, Charles R.; de Cristo-Araújo, Michelly; d'Eeckenbrugge, Geo Coppens; Alves Pereira, Alessandro; Picanço-Rodrigues, Doriane (6 January 2010). "Origin and Domestication of Native Amazonian Crops". Diversity 2

Compendium of medicinal plants. (2004). Delhi, India: National Institute of Industrial Research.

Commission E monographs. (1998). American Botanical Council.

Committee on Comparative Toxicity of Naturally Occurring Carcinogens, Board on Environmental Studies and Toxicology, Commission on Life Sciences, and National Research Council (1996). Carcinogens and anticarcinogens in the human diet: a comparison of naturally occurring and synthetic substances. National Academy Press, Washington, D.C.

Conti B., Canale A., Bertoli A., Gozzini F., Pistelli L. Essential oil composition and larvicidal activity of six Mediterranean aromatic plants against the mosquito Aedes albopictus (Diptera: Culicidae). Parasitology Research 2010

Coombes, A. (1985). Dictionary of plant names. Portland, Or.: Timber Press.

Coon JT, Ernst E. Andrographis paniculata: a systematic review of safety and efficacy, Planta, 2004

Coon, N. (1977). The dictionary of useful plants. Emmaus: Roodale Press.

Culpepers British Herbal - Pub. William Nicholson and Son - C. 1905 (re-print of the 1653 original)

Cummings, D., & Holmes, A. (n.d.). The medicinal gardening handbook: A complete guide to growing, harvesting, and using healing herbs.

Dasanayake, Ananda P.; Silverman, Amanda J.; Warnakulasuriya, Saman (2010). "Maté drinking and oral and oro-pharyngeal cancer: A systematic review and meta-analysis". Oral Oncology 46

Davidson, A. (1999). The Oxford companion to food. Oxford: Oxford University Press.

Davis & Company Parke (1909). Manual of therapeutics. Parke, Davis & Co.

Davydov M, Krikorian AD. (October 2000). "Eleutherococcus senticosus (Rupr. & Maxim.) Maxim. (Araliaceae) as an adaptogen: a closer look". Journal of Ethnopharmacology 72

de Mesquita, M., et al. "Cytotoxic activity of Brazilian Cerrado plants used in traditional medicine against cancer cell lines." J Ethnopharmacol. 2009

de Lourdes Arruzazabala, M.; Molina, V.; Más, R.; Carbajal, D.; Marrero, D.;

González, V.; Rodríguez, E. (2007). "Effects of coconut oil on testosterone-induced prostatic hyperplasia in Sprague-Dawley rats". Journal of Pharmacy and Pharmacology 59

Dedhia RC, McVary KT (June 2008). "Phytotherapy for lower urinary tract symptoms secondary to benign prostatic hyperplasia". J. Urol. 179 (6): 2119–2125.

Dekosky, S. T.; Williamson, J. D.; Fitzpatrick, A. L.; Kronmal, R. A.; Ives, D. G.; Saxton, J. A.; Lopez, O. L.; Burke, G. et al. (2008). "Ginkgo biloba for Prevention of Dementia: A Randomized Controlled Trial". Journal of the American Medical Association 300

Devi, P. U.; Ganasoundari, A. (March 1999). "Modulation of glutathione and antioxidant enzymes by Ocimum sanctum and its role in protection against radiation injury". Indian Journal of Experimental Biology 37

Dew, Tristan P.; Day, Andrea J.; Morgan, Michael R. A. (2005). "Xanthine Oxidase Activity in Vitro: Effects of Food Extracts and Components". Journal of Agricultural and Food Chemistry 53

Dhama, K., & Dhama, S. (1994). Homoeopathy: The complete handbook. New Delhi: UBS ' Distributors. Complete Homeopathy Handbook 1996 Castro

Dictionary catalog of the National Agricultural Library, 1862-1965. (1967). New York: Rowman and Littlefield.

Djavan B, Fong YK, Chaudry A, et al. (2005). "Progression delay in men with mild symptoms of bladder outlet obstruction: a comparative study of phytotherapy and watchful waiting". World J Urol 23 (4): 253–6.

Dos, Santos-Neto, Ll; De, Vilhena, Toledo, Ma; Medeiros-Souza, P; De,

Souza, Ga (December 2006). "The use of herbal medicine in Alzheimer's disease-a systematic review" (Free full text). Evidence-based complementary and alternative medicine : eCAM 3

Drugs and Supplements. (n.d.). Retrieved from http://www.mayoclinic.org/drugs-supplements

Duke, J. (1992). Handbook of edible weeds. Boca Raton: CRC Press.

Duke, J. (2000). The green pharmacy herbal handbook: Your comprehensive reference to the best herbs for healing. Emmaus, Pa.: Rodale Reach

Duke. J. A. and Ayensu. E. S. Medicinal Plants of China. Reference Publications, Inc. 1985

Dumitru, Alina F.; Shamji, Mohamed; Wagenmann, Martin; Hindersin, Simone; Scheckenbach, Kathrin; Greve, Jens; Klenzner, Thomas; Hess, Lorenzo et al. (2011). "Petasol butenoate complex (Ze 339) relieves allergic rhinitis–induced nasal obstruction more effectively than desloratadine". Journal of Allergy and Clinical Immunology 127

Ebadi, M. (2002). Pharmacodynamic basis of herbal medicine. Boca Raton, Fla.: CRC Press.

Ebadi, M., & Ebadi, M. (2008). Desk reference of clinical pharmacology (2nd ed.). Boca Raton: CRC Press.

Ebrahimi, Sedigheh; Soheil Ashkani Esfahani, Azizollah Poormahmudi. (2011). "Investigating the efficacy of Zizyphus jujuba on neonatal jaundice". Iranian Journal of Pediatrics 21

Edes, R. (1883). Therapeutic handbook of the United States pharmacopoeia: Being a condensed statement of the physiological and toxic action, medicinal value, methods of administration and doses of the drugs and preparations in the latest edition of the U.S. pharmacopoeia ... New York: William Wood and.

El Bardai S, Lyoussi B, Wibo M, Morel N (May 2001). "Pharmacological evidence of hypotensive activity of Marrubium vulgare and Foeniculum vulgare in spontaneously hypertensive rat". Clin. Exp. Hypertens. 23

Elsabagh, Sarah; Hartley, David E.; Ali, Osama; Williamson, Elizabeth M.; File, Sandra E. (2005). "Differential cognitive effects of Ginkgo biloba after acute and chronic treatment in healthy young volunteers". Psychopharmacology 179

Erichsen-Brown, Charlotte (1989). Medicinal and Other Uses of North American Plants: A Historical Survey with Special Reference to the Eastern Indian Tribes. Dover Publications

Erika Svangård, Ulf Göransson, Zozan Hocaoglu, Joachim Gullbo, Rolf Larsson,, Per Claeson and Lars Bohlin, 2004. "Cytotoxic Cyclotides from Viola tricolor" Journal of Natural Products 67 Estrogen-like activity of ginsenoside Rg1 derived from Panax notoginseng". The Journal of Clinical Endocrinology and Metabolism 87

Ettefagh K.A., Burns J.T., Junio H.A., Kaatz G.W., Cech N.B., "Goldenseal (Hydrastis canadensis L.) Extracts Synergistically Enhance the Antibacterial Activity of Berberine via Efflux Pump Inhibition", Planta Medica 2010

Evans, P. (1961). A modern herbal. San Francisco: Porpoise Bookshop.

A Modern Herbal 1931 Grieve

Ewing, G. (1971). Topics in chemical instrumentation; a volume of reprints from the Journal of chemical education. Easton, Pa.: Chemical Education Pub.

Facciola, S. (1998). Cornucopia II: A source book of edible plants. Vista, CA: Kampong Publications.

Farag RS. Chemical and biological evaluation of the essential oils of different Melaleuca species. Phytother Res. Jan2004;18(1):30-35.

Lee CK. A new norlupene from the leaves of Melaleuca leucadendron. J Nat Prod.

Farnsworth, N. R.; Draus, F. J.; Sager, R. W.; Bianculli, J. A. (2006). "Studies on Vinca major L. (Apocynaceae) I. Isolation of perivincine". Journal of the American Pharmaceutical Association 49

Fehske, Christian J.; Leuner, Kristina; Müller, Walter E. (2009). "Ginkgo biloba extract (EGb761®) influences monoaminergic neurotransmission via inhibition of NE uptake, but not MAO activity after chronic treatment". Pharmacological Research 60

Fern, K. Plants for a Future: Edible and Useful Plants for a Healthier World. Hampshire: Permanent Publications, 1997.

Fernández S, Wasowski C, Paladini AC, Marder M (2004). "Sedative and sleep-enhancing properties of linarin, a flavonoid-isolated from Valeriana officinalis". Pharmacol Biochem Behav 77

Figueirinha A. Cruz MT. Francisco V. Lopes MC. Batista MT. Anti-inflammatory activity of Cymbopogon citratus leaf infusion in lipopolysaccharide-stimulated dendritic cells: contribution of the polyphenols. Journal of Medicinal Food. 13

Figueroa A, Sanchez-Gonzalez MA, Wong A, Arjmandi BH (2012). "Watermelon extract supplementation reduces ankle blood pressure and carotid augmentation index in obese adults with prehypertension or hypertension". American journal of hypertension 25

Filip, Rosana; Lotito, Silvina B.; Ferraro, Graciela; Fraga, Cesar G. (2000). "Antioxidant activity of Ilex paraguariensis and related species". Nutrition Research 20

Foster, S., & Duke, J. (1990). A field guide to medicinal plants: Eastern and central North America. Boston: Houghton Mifflin.

Francois, G., et al. "Antimalarial and cytotoxic potential of four quassinoids from Hannoa chlorantha and Hannoa klaineana, and their structure-activity relationships." Int. J. Parasitol. 1998

Fu, P.P., Yang, Y.C., Xia, Q., Chou, M.C., Cui, Y.Y., Lin G., "Pyrrolizidine alkaloids-tumorigenic components in Chinese herbal medicines and dietary supplements", Journal of Food and Drug Analysis, Vol. 10, No. 4, 2002

Fugh-Berman, Adriane (2000). "Herb-drug interactions". The Lancet 355

Furst, Peter T. (1976). Hallucinogens and Culture. Chandler & Sharp.

Gadang, V; Gilbert, W; Hettiararchchy, N; Horax, R; Katwa, L; Devareddy, L (2011). "Dietary bitter melon seed increases peroxisome proliferator-activated receptor-γ gene expression in adipose tissue, down-regulates the nuclear factor-κB expression, and alleviates the symptoms associated with metabolic syndrome". Journal of medicinal food 14

Gadow, A.Von; Joubert, E.; Hansmann, C.F. (1997). "Comparison of the antioxidant activity of rooibos tea (Aspalathus linearis) with green, oolong and black tea". Food Chemistry 60

Gaginella, T. (1997). Biochemical pharmacology as an approach to gastrointestinal disorders: Basic science to clinical perspectives (1996) : IUPHAR GI Pharmacology Symposium. Dordrecht: Kluwer Academic.

Ganzera M, Aberham A, Stuppner H (May 2006). "Development and validation of an HPLC/UV/MS method for simultaneous determination of 18 preservatives in grapefruit seed extract". J. Agric. Food Chem. 54

Gautam M. Saha S. Bani S. Kaul A. Mishra S. Patil D. Satti NK. Suri KA. Gairola S. Suresh K. Jadhav S. Qazi GN. Patwardhan B. Immunomodulatory activity of Asparagus racemosus on systemic Th1/Th2 immunity: implications for immunoadjuvant potential. Journal of Ethnopharmacology. 121

Grae, I. (1974). Nature's colors; dyes from plants. New York: Macmillan.

Gray, A., & Sullivant, W. (1848). A manual of the botany of the northern United States from New England to Wisconsin and south to Ohio and Pennsylvania inclusive: (the mosses and liverworts by Wm. S. Sullivant,) arranged according to the natural system. Boston: J. Munroe.

Geller SE, Shulman LP, van Breemen RB, et al. (2009). "Safety and efficacy of black cohosh and red clover for the management of vasomotor symptoms: a randomized controlled trial". Menopause (New York, N.Y.) 16

Genders. R. Scented Flora of the World. Robert Hale. London. 1994

Gentry EJ, Jampani HB, Keshavarz-Shokri A, et al. (October 1998). "Antitubercular natural products: berberine from the roots of commercial Hydrastis canadensis powder. Isolation of inactive 8-oxotetrahydrothalifendine, canadine, beta-hydrastine, and two new quinic acid esters, hycandinic acid esters-1 and -2". Journal of Natural Products 61

Germplasm Resources Information Network. United States Department of Agriculture. 1997-05-22. Retrieved 2010-04-12.

Ghalayini IF, Al-Ghazo MA, Harfeil MN 2011. Prophylaxis and therapeutic effects of raspberry (Rubus idaeus) on renal stone formation in Balb/c mice. Int Braz J Urol. 37

Ghosh, P. C., et al. "Antitumor plants. IV. Constituents of Simarouba versicolor." Lloydia. 1977

Ghosh S, Sharma AK, Kumar S, Tiwari SS, Rastogi S, Srivastava S, Singh M, Kumar R, Paul S, Ray DD, Rawat AK "In vitro and in vivo efficacy of Acorus calamus extract against Rhipicephalus (Boophilus) microplus." Parasitol Res. 2011

Gião MS, Pestana D, Faria A, Guimarães JT, Pintado ME, Calhau C, Azevedo I, Malcata FX., 2010. Effects of extracts of selected medicinal plants upon hepatic oxidative stress. Journal Medicinal Food. 13

Gibbs A, Green C, Doctor VM. (1983). "Isolation and anticoagulant properties of polysaccharides of Typha Augustata and Daemonorops species". Thromb Res. 32

Gilani A.H., Bashir S., Khan A.-u."Pharmacological basis for the use of Borago officinalis in gastrointestinal, respiratory and cardiovascular disorders". Journal of Ethnopharmacology. 114

Giles M., Ulbricht C., Khalsa K.P.S., DeFranco Kirkwood C., Park C., Basch E., "Butterbur: An evidence-based systematic review by the natural standard research collaboration Journal of Herbal Pharmacotherapy 2005

God J, Tate PL, Larcom LL 2010. Red raspberries have antioxidant effects that play a minor role in the killing of stomach and colon cancer cells. Nutritional Research. 30

Godevac D, Tesević V, Vajs V, Milosavljević S, Stanković M., 2009. Antioxidant properties of raspberry seed extracts on micronucleus distribution in peripheral blood lymphocytes. Food Chem 47

Godowski, KC (1989). "Antimicrobial action of sanguinarine". The Journal of clinical dentistry 1

Golshahi H., Ghasemi E., Mehranzade E. (2011). "Antibacterial activity of Ocimum sanctum extract against E. coli, S. aureus and P. aeruginosa". Clinical Biochemistry. Conference: 12th Iranian Congress of Biochemistry, ICB and 4th International Congress of Biochemistry and Molecular Biology 44

Goodner, K.L. et al.; Mahattanatawee, K; Plotto, A; Sotomayor, J; Jordan, M (2006). "Aromatic profiles of Thymus hyemalis and Spanish T. vulgaris essential oils by GC–MS/GC–O". Industrial Crops and Products 24

Gregory PJ, Sperry M, Wilson AF (January 2008). "Dietary supplements for osteoarthritis". Am Fam Physician 77

Grieve, M. (1971). A modern herbal; the medicinal, culinary, cosmetic and economic properties, cultivation and folk-lore of herbs, grasses, fungi, shrubs, & trees with all their modern scientific uses,. New York: Dover Publications.

Griffith, J.Q.; J.F. Couch, M. A. Lindauer (1944). "Effect of Rutin on Increased Capillary Fragility". Proc Soc Exp Biol Med March 55

Grover, J. K.; Yadav, S. P. (2004). "Pharmacological actions and potential uses of Momordica charantia: A review". Journal of Ethnopharmacology 93

Grubben, G.J.H. & Denton, O.A. (2004) Plant Resources of Tropical Africa 2. Vegetables. PROTA Foundation, Wageningen; Backhuys, Leiden; CTA, Wageningen

Grujic-Jovanovic S., Skaltsa H.D., Marin P., Sokovic M. "Composition and antibacterial activity of the essential oil of six Stachys species from Serbia" Flavour and Fragrance Journal 2004 19

Gualtiero Simonetti (1990). Stanley Schuler, ed. Simon & Schuster's Guide to Herbs and Spices. Simon & Schuster, Inc.

Gualtiero Simonetti (1990). Stanley Schuler, ed. Simon & Schuster's Guide to Herbs and Spices. Simon & Schuster, Inc.

Guenther, E. (1949). The essential oils. New York: D. Van Nostrand.

Guo LY. Hung TM. Bae KH. Shin EM. Zhou HY. Hong YN. Kang SS. Kim HP. Kim YS.,"Anti-inflammatory effects of schisandrin isolated from the fruit of Schisandra chinensis Baill." European Journal of Pharmacology. 591

Guo, R; Pittler, MH; Ernst, E (2007). "Herbal medicines for the treatment of allergic rhinitis: A systematic review". Annals of allergy, asthma & immunology : official publication of the American College of Allergy, Asthma, & Immunology 99

Gurudeeban, S.; Satyavani K., Ramanathan T. (2010). "Bitter Apple (Citrullus colocynthis): An Overview of Chemical Composition and Biomedical Potentials". Asian Journal of Plant Sciences 9

H. J. D. Dorman and S. G. Deans (2000). "Antimicrobial agents from plants: antibacterial activity of plant volatile oils". Journal of Applied Microbiology 88

H. Kohno, Y. Yasui, R. Suzuki, M. Hosokawa, K. Miyashita, T. Tanaka (2004), Dietary seed oil rich in conjugated linolenic acid from bitter melon inhibits azoxymethane-induced rat colon carcinogenesis through elevation of colonic PPAR γ expression and alteration of lipid composition. International Journal of Cancer, volume 110

Ha H.H., Park S.Y., Ko W.S., Kim Y. "Gleditsia sinensis thorns inhibit the production of NO through NF-B suppression in LPS-stimulated macrophages. Journal of Ethnopharmacology. 2008. 118

Hage-Sleiman, R; Mroueh, M; Daher, CF (2011). "Pharmacological evaluation of aqueous extract of Althaea officinalis flower grown in Lebanon". Pharmaceutical biology 49

Hager TJ, Howard LR, Liyanage R, Lay JO, Prior RL (February 2008). "Ellagitannin composition of blackberry as determined by HPLC-ESI-MS and MALDI-TOF-MS". Journal of Agricultural and Food Chemistry 56

Halvorsen BL, Carlsen MH, Phillips KM, et al. (July 2006). "Content of redox-active compounds (ie, antioxidants) in foods consumed in the United States". The American Journal of Clinical Nutrition 84

Hamamelitannin from Witch Hazel (Hamamelis virginiana) Displays Specific Cytotoxic Activity against Colon Cancer Cells. Susana Sánchez-Tena, María L. Fernández-Cachón, Anna Carreras, M. Luisa Mateos-Martín, Noelia Costoya, Mary P. Moyer, María J. Nuñez, Josep L. Torres and Marta Cascante, J. Nat. Prod.

Hammer, K; Carson, C; Riley, T; Nielsen, J (2006). "A review of the toxicity of Melaleuca alternifolia (tea tree) oil". Food and Chemical Toxicology 44

Hanelt, Peter; Büttner, R.; Mansfeld, Rudolf; Kilian, Ruth (2001). Mansfeld's Encyclopedia of Agricultural and Horticultural Crops. Springer.

Hannan JM. Marenah L. Ali L. Rokeya B. Flatt PR. Abdel-Wahab YH. Insulin secretory actions of extracts of Asparagus racemosus root in perfused pancreas, isolated islets and clonal pancreatic beta-cells. Journal of Endocrinology. 192

Harborne, J. (1996). Dictionary of plant toxins. Chichester: Wiley.

Harper, Douglas; Online Etymological Dictionary; http://www.etymonline.com/index

Harrison, Lorraine (2012). RHS Latin for gardeners. United Kingdom: Mitchell Beazley.

Haskell CF, Kennedy DO, Wesnes KA, Milne AL, Scholey AB (January 2007). "A double-blind, placebo-controlled, multi-dose evaluation of the acute behavioral effects of guaraná in humans". J. Psychopharmacol. (Oxford) 21

Hartwell, Jonathan L. (1971). Bioactive Plants "Plants used against cancer. A survey". Lloydia

Hausen, B. M. (1993). "Centella asiatica (Indian pennywort), an effective therapeutic but a weak sensitizer". Contact Dermatitis 29 (

Hecht SS, Carmella SG, Murphy SE (1 October 1999). "Effects of watercress consumption on urinary metabolites of nicotine in smokers". Cancer Epidemiol Biomarkers

Heinonen, M (2007). "Antioxidant activity and antimicrobial effect of berry phenolics--a Finnish perspective". Molecular nutrition & food research 51

Heinrich, Clark (2002). Magic Mushrooms in Religion and Alchemy. Rochester: Park Street Press.

Heisy, Rod M. (May 1990). "Allelopathic and Herbicidal Effects of Extracts from Tree of Heaven". American Journal of Botany 77

Henrotin Y, Clutterbuck AL, Allaway D, et al. (February 2010). "Biological actions of curcumin on articular chondrocytes". Osteoarthr. Cartil. 18

Hensel, Andreas; Maas, Mareike; Sendker, Jandirk; Lechtenberg, Matthias; Petereit, Frank; Deters, Alexandra; Schmidt, Thomas & Stark, Timo (2011). "Eupatorium perfoliatum L.: Phytochemistry, traditional use and current applications". Journal of Ethnopharmacology

Herbal therapy, medicinal plants, and natural products: An IPA compilation. (1999). Bethesda, MD: American Society of Health-System Pharmacists.

Herbs and natural supplements: An evidence based guide. (n.d.). Mosby Sydney, Australia.

Hess AM, Sullivan DL (2005). "Potential for toxicity with use of bitter orange extract and guarana for weight loss". The Annals of pharmacotherapy 39

Heywood VH. 1993 "Flowering plants of the world." Oxford University Press, New York

Hillier & Sons. (1977). Hilliers' Manual of Trees and Shrubs, 4th Edition. David & Charles, Newton Abbot, England.

Hirota, N. and Hiroi, M., 1967. 'The later studies on the camphor tree, on the leaf oil of each practical form and its utilisation', Perfumery and Essential Oil Record 58

Hirsch, Pamela; Gladstar, Rosemary (2000). Planting the future: saving our medicinal herbs. Rochester, Vt: Healing Arts Press

Hoa NK, Phan DV, Thuan ND, Ostenson CG (April 2009). "Screening of the hypoglycemic effect of eight Vietnamese herbal drugs". Methods & Findings in Experimental & Clinical Pharmacology 31

Hoffmann, Medical Herbalism: Principles and Practices, Healing Arts Press, 2003

Holliday, P. (1989). A dictionary of plant pathology. Cambridge [England: Cambridge University Press.

Holzl J, Godau P. (1989). "Receptor binding studies with Valeriana officinalis on the benzodiazepine receptor". Planta Medica 55

Hong B; Ji YH; Hong JH; Nam KY; Ahn TY A double-blind crossover study evaluating the efficacy of korean red ginseng in patients with erectile dysfunction: a preliminary report. J Urol. 2002

Huang L.-Z., Huang B.-K., Ye Q., Qin L.-P. "Bioactivity-guided fractionation for anti-fatigue property of Acanthopanax senticosus" Journal of Ethnopharmacology 2011

Huang Yuan, Dong Qi, Qiao Shan-Yi. Studies on the Chemical Constituents From Stellaria media (II). Pharmaceutical Journal of Chinese People's Liberation Army, 2007-03 (abstract) (Article in Chinese)

Hughes, R. Elwyn; Ellery, Peter; Harry, Tim; Jenkins, Vivian; Jones, Eleri (1980). "The dietary potential of the common nettle". Journal of the Science of Food and Agriculture 31

Hunt EJ, Lester CE, Lester EA, Tackett RL. (June 2001). "Effect of St. John's wort on free radical production". Life Sci. 69

Hutchens, A. (1992). A handbook of native American herbs. Boston: [New York]

Huxley, A., ed. (1992). New RHS Dictionary of Gardening. Macmillan

Huyen VT, Phan DV, Thang P, Hoa NK, Ostenson CG (May 2010). "Antidiabetic effect of Gynostemma pentaphyllum tea in randomly assigned type 2 diabetic patients". Hormone & Metabolic Research 42

Iacobellis, N S. et al. (2005). "Antibacterial Activity of Cuminum cyminum L. and Carum carvi L. Essential Oils". Journal of Agricultural and Food Chemistry 53

Index herbariorum. (1990). Bronx, N.Y.: Published and distributed for International Association for Plant Taxonomy by New York Botanical Gardens.

Indian journal of natural products. (1985). Sagar, India: [Indian Society of Pharmacognosy].

ISHS Acta Horticulturae 306: International Symposium on Medicinal and Aromatic Plants, XXIII IHC

Isolation and purification of baicalein, wogonin and oroxylin A from the medicinal plant Scutellaria baicalensis by high-speed counter-current chromatography. Hua-Bin Li and Feng Chen, Journal of Chromatography A, 2005, Volume 1074

Ital J Biochem. 1988. Effect of the triterpenoid fraction of Centella asiatica on macromolecules of the connective matrix in human skin fibroblast cultures. Tenni R, Zanaboni G, De Agostini MP, Rossi A, Bendotti C, Cetta G.

Izzo A.A. Ernst E. (2001). "Interactions Between Herbal Medicines and Prescribed Drugs: A Systematic Review". Drugs (Adis International) 61

J. Östman; M. Britton, eds. (2004), "4.7.3 Alternative Medicine Methods Used to Treat Obesity", Treating and Preventing Obesity: An Evidence Based Review, Wiley-VCH.

Jarald E., Nalwaya N., Sheeja E., Ahmad S., Jamalludin S. (2010). "Comparative study on diuretic activity of few medicinal plants in individual form and in combination form". Indian Drugs 47

Jedličková Z. Antibacterial properties of the Vietnamese cajeput oil and ocimum oil in combination with antibacterial agents. J Hyg Epidemiol Microbiol Immunol.

Jeong-Kyu KIM, Chang-Soo KANG, Jong-Kwon LEE, Young-Ran KIM, Hye-Yun HAN, Hwa Kyung YUN (2005). "Evaluation of Repellency Effect of Two Natural Aroma Mosquito Repellent Compounds, Citronella and Citronellal". Entomological Research 35

Jiang J.-G., Huang X.-J., Chen J., Lin Q.-S.,"Comparison of the sedative and hypnotic effects of flavonoids, saponins, and polysaccharides extracted from Semen Ziziphus jujube" Natural Produ ct Research 2007 21

Jigna Parekh, Nehal Karathia, Sumitra Chanda (2006). "Screening of some traditionally used medicinal plants for potential antibacterial activity". Indian Journal of Pharmaceutical Sciences 68

Jing, M. et al. (1987). "Study on the mechanism of Valeriana officinalis for infantile viral diarrhea". Yunnan J. Traditional Chin. Med. 8

Jordan P; Wheeler S. (2001). The ultimate mushroom book. Hermes House.

Joseph I. Boullata and Angela M. Nace (2000). "Safety Issues with Herbal Medicine: Common Herbal Medicines". Pharmacotherapy 20

Joubert, E.; Gelderblom, W.C.A.; Louw, A.; De Beer, D. (2008). "South African herbal teas: Aspalathus linearis, Cyclopia spp. And Athrixia phylicoides—A review". Journal of Ethnopharmacology 119

Jung HA, Su BN, Keller WJ, Mehta RG, Kinghorn AD (March 2006). "Antioxidant xanthones from the pericarp of Garcinia mangostana (Mangosteen)". Journal of Agricultural and Food Chemistry 54

Jung S.M., Schumacher H.R., Kim H., Kim M., Lee S.H., Pessler F. "Reduction of urate crystal-induced inflammation by root extracts from traditional oriental medicinal plants: Elevation of prostaglandin D2levels" Arthritis Research and Therapy 2007 9

Junwei J. Zhu, Christopher A. Dunlap, Robert W. Behle, Dennis R. Berkebile, Brian Wienhold. (2010). Repellency of a wax-based catnip-oil formulation against stable flies. Journal of Agricultural and Food Chemistry, 58

Kade, F.; Miller, W. (1993). "Dose-dependent effects of Ginkgo biloba extraction on cerebral, mental and physical efficiency: a placebo controlled double blind study". British journal of clinical research 4.

Kamal-Eldin A, Moazzami A, Washi S (January 2011). "Sesame seed lignans: potent physiological modulators and possible ingredients in functional foods & nutraceuticals". Recent Pat Food Nutr Agric 3

Kamaldeep Dhawan, Suresh Kumar, Anupam Sharma (2001). "Anti-anxiety studies on extracts of Passiflora incarnata Linneaus [sic]". Journal of Ethnopharmacology 78

Kamaldeep Dhawan & Anupam Sharma (2002). "Antitussive activity of the methanol extract of Passiflora incarnata leaves". Fitoterapia 73 Kamaldeep Dhawan, Suresh Kumar & Anupam Sharma (2003). "Antiasthmatic activity of the methanol extract of leaves of Passiflora incarnata". Phytotherapy Research 17

Kamat JP. Boloor KK. Devasagayam TP. Venkatachalam SR. Antioxidant properties of Asparagus racemosus against damage induced by gamma-radiation in rat liver mitochondria. Journal of Ethnopharmacology. 71

Kamdem D. P., Gage, D. A. (1995). "Chemical Composition of Essential Oil from the Root Bark of Sassafras albidum". Journal of Organic Chemistry 61

Kang IJ, Lee MH (July 2006). "Quantification of para-phenylenediamine and heavy metals in henna dye". Contact Dermatitis 55

Kanwar, Anubha Singh ; Bhutani, Kamlesh Kumar "Effects of Chlorophytum arundinaceum, Asparagus adscendens and Asparagus racemosus on Pro-inflammatory Cytokine and Corticosterone Levels Produced by Stress" . BIOSIS Previews Phytotherapy Research. 24

Kapasakalidis, PG; Rastall, RA; Gordon, MH (2006). "Extraction of polyphenols from processed black currant (Ribes nigrum L.) residues". Journal of Agricultural and Food Chemistry 54

Katsaridis, V.; Papagiannaki C., Aimar E. (2009). "Embolization of brain arteriovenous malformations for cure: because we could and because we should". American Journal of Neuroradiology 30

Katzenschlager, R; Evans, A; Manson, A; Patsalos, PN; Ratnaraj, N; Watt, H; Timmermann, L; Van Der Giessen, R et al. (2004). "Mucuna pruriens in Parkinson's disease: a double blind clinical and pharmacological study". Journal of Neurology, Neurosurgery & Psychiatry 75

Kaufman, PB; Duke, JA; Brielmann, H; Boik, J; Hoyt, JE (1997). "A comparative survey of leguminous plants as sources of the isoflavones, genistein and daidzein: Implications for human nutrition and health". Journal of alternative and complementary medicine 3 Kaunitz, H. (1986). "Medium chain triglycerides (MCT) in aging and arteriosclerosis". Journal of Environmental Pathology, Toxicology and Oncology : official organ of the International Society for Environmental Toxicology and Cancer 6

Kennedy, D. O.; Little, W; Scholey, AB (2004). "Attenuation of Laboratory-Induced Stress in Humans After Acute Administration of Melissa officinalis (Lemon Balm)". Psychosomatic Medicine 66

Khan MR , Omoloso AD . Antibacterial activity of Hygrophila stricta and Peperomia pellucida . Fitoterapia . 2002

Khonkarn R. Okonogi S. Ampasavate C. Anuchapreeda S. Investigation of fruit peel extracts as sources for compounds with antioxidant and antiproliferative activities against human cell lines. Food & Chemical Toxicology. 48

Kilham, C. (2000). Tales from the Medicine Trail: Tracking Down the Health Secrets of Shamans, Herbalists, Mystics, Yogis, and Other Healers. [Emmaus PA]: Rodale Press.

Kim, H.; Song, M-J.; Potter, D. (2005). "Medicinal efficacy of plants utilized as temple food in traditional Korean

Buddihsm". Journal of Ethnopharmacology 104

Kim, H. J.; Chang, E. J.; Cho, S. H.; Chung, S. K.; Park, H. D.; Choi, S. W. (2002). "Antioxidative activity of resveratrol and its derivatives isolated from seeds of Paeonia lactiflora". Bioscience, biotechnology, and biochemistry 66

Kim, M. H.; Nugroho, A.; Choi, J.; Park, J. H.; Park, H. J. (2011). "Rhododendrin, an analgesic/anti-inflammatory arylbutanoid glycoside, from the leaves of Rhododendron aureum". Archives of Pharmacal Research 34

Kim SJ. Min HY. Lee EJ. Kim YS. Bae K. Kang SS. Lee SK. 'Growth inhibition and cell cycle arrest in the G0/G1 by schizandrin, a dibenzocyclooctadiene lignan isolated from Schisandra chinensis, on T47D human breast cancer cells." Phytotherapy Research. 24

King, J., & Felter, H. (1898). King's American dispensatory (18th ed.). Cincinnati: Ohio Valley

Klepser TB, Klepser ME (1999). "Unsafe and potentially safe herbal therapies". Am J Health-Syst Pharm 56

Ko HC, Wei BL, Chiou WF. The effect of medicinal plants used in Chinese folk medicine on RANTES, Ethnopharmacol, 2006

Koh, H., & Chua, T. (2009). A guide to medicinal plants an illustrated, scientific and medicinal approach. Singapore: World Scientific Pub.

Kraemer, H. (1910). A text-book of botany and pharmacognosy, intended for the use of students of pharmacy, as a reference book for pharmacists, and as a handbook for food and drug analysts, (4th rev. and enl. ed.). Philadelphia & London: J.B. Lippincott Company.

Krafczyk, Nicole; Woyand, Franziska; Glomb, Marcus A. (2009). "Structure-antioxidant relationship of flavonoids from fermented rooibos". Molecular Nutrition & Food Research 53

Krochmal, A., & Krochmal, C. (1984). A field guide to medicinal plants (Updated Times Books pbk. ed.). New York, N.Y.: Times Books.

Kang IJ, Lee MH (July 2006). "Quantification of para-phenylenediamine and heavy metals in henna dye". Contact Dermatitis 55

Kulkarni AP, Mahal HS, Kapoor S, Aradhya SM (February 21, 2007). "In vitro studies on the binding, antioxidant, and cytotoxic actions of punicalagin". J Agric Food Chem 55

Kumar, S. (1998). A complete clinical handbook for every day practice. New Delhi: Indian Books & Periodicals.

Kumar S., Singh Y. V., & Singh, M. (2005). "Agro-History, Uses, Ecology and Distribution of Henna (Lawsonia inermis L. syn. Alba Lam)". Henna: Cultivation, Improvement, and Trade. Jodhpur: Central Arid Zone Research Institute.

Kunkel SD, Elmore CJ, Bongers KS, Ebert SM, Fox DK, et al. (2012) Ursolic Acid Increases Skeletal Muscle and Brown Fat and Decreases Diet-Induced Obesity, Glucose Intolerance and Fatty Liver Disease. PLoS ONE 7

Kurkin VA, Dubishchev AV, Ezhkov VN, Titova IN, Avdeeva EV (2006). "Antidepressant activity of some phytopharmaceuticals and phenylpropanoids". Pharmaceutical Chemistry Journal 40

L. Kumar P., Sharma B., Bakshi N.,"Biological activity of alkaloids from Solanum dulcamara". Natural Product Research. 23. 2009.

Larrosa M, González-Sarrías A, Yáñez-Gascón MJ, Selma MV, Azorín-Ortuño

M, Toti S, Tomás-Barberán F, Dolara P, Espín JC (19 July 2009). "Anti-inflammatory properties of a pomegranate extract and its metabolite urolithin-A in a colitis rat model and the effect of colon inflammation on phenolic metabolism". J Nutr Biochem 21

Lauro, Gabriel J.; Francis, F. Jack (2000). Natural Food Colorants Science and Technology. IFT Basic Symposium Series. New York: Marcel Dekker.

Galindo-Cuspinera, V; Westhoff, DC; Rankin, SA (2003). "Antimicrobial properties of commercial annatto extracts against selected pathogenic, lactic acid, and spoilage microorganisms". Journal of food protection 66

Lawrence, B. M., 1995. 'Progress in essential oils', Perfumer and Flavorist, "Leaf Extract Treatment During the Growth Spurt Period Enhances Hippocampal CA3 Neuronal Dendritic Arborization in Rats". Evid Based Complement Alternat Med: 2006.

Lee do Y. Choo BK. Yoon T. Cheon MS. Lee HW. Lee AY. Kim HK. Anti-inflammatory effects of Asparagus cochinchinensis extract in acute and chronic cutaneous inflammation. Journal of Ethnopharmacology. 121

Lee HJ. Jeong HS. Kim DJ. Noh YH. Yuk DY. Hong JT. Inhibitory effect of citral on NO production by suppression of iNOS expression and NF-kappa B activation in RAW264.7 cells. Archives of Pharmacal Research. 31

Lee IA, Joh EH, Kim DH, "Arctigenin Isolated from the Seeds of Arctium lappa Ameliorates Memory Deficits in Mice." Planta Med. 2011

Lee M.-Y., Shin I.-S., Seo C.-S., Ha H., Shin H.-K."Antiasthmatic effects of Gleditsia sinensis in an ovalbumin-induced murine model of asthma". International Journal of Toxicology. 30. 2011

Lee S.-J., Park K., Ha S.-D., Kim W.-J., Moon S.-K. " Gleditsia sinensis thorn extract inhibits human colon cancer cells: The role of ERK1/2, G2/M-phase cell cycle arrest and p53 expression". Phytotherapy Research. 24

Lee, Seung-Joo et al.; Umano, K; Shibamoto, T; Lee, K (2005). "Identification of volatile components in basil (Ocimum basilicum L.) and thyme leaves (Thymus vulgaris L.) and their antioxidant properties". Food Chemistry 91

Lee, YJ; Jin, YR; Lim, WC; Park, WK; Cho, JY; Jang, S; Lee, SK (2003). "Ginsenoside-Rb1 acts as a weak phytoestrogen in MCF-7 human breast cancer cells". Archives of pharmacal research 26

Leite JR, Seabra Mde L, Maluf E, et al. (July 1986). "Pharmacology of lemongrass (Cymbopogon citratus Stapf). III. Assessment of eventual toxic, hypnotic and anxiolytic effects on humans". J Ethnopharmacol 17

Leos-Rivas C., Verde-Star M.J., Torres L.O., Oranday-Cardenas A., Rivas-Morales C., Barron-Gonzalez M.P., Morales-Vallarta M.R., Cruz-Vega D.E. In vitro amoebicidal activity of borage (Borago officinalis) extract on entamoeba histolytica. Journal of Medicinal Food. 14. 2011.

Lesca, P. (1983). Protective effects of ellagic acid and other plant phenols on benzo[a]pyrene-induced neoplasia in mice.

Lewis K (April 2001). "In search of natural substrates and inhibitors of MDR pumps". Journal of Molecular Microbiology and Biotechnology 3

Lewis, WH and Elvin-Lewis, MPF (2003). Medical botany: plants affecting human health. Hoboken, New Jersey; John Wiley & Sons

Li, C. (1974). Chinese herbal medicine. Washington: U.S. Dept. of Health, Education, and Welfare, Public Health Service, National Institutes of Health.

Li, C. (2003). Chinese herbal medicine. San Diego, Calif.: Book Tree.

Li, Tao; Zhang, Hao (2008), "Identification and Comparative Determination of Rhodionin in Traditional Tibetan Medicinal Plants of Fourteen Rhodiola Species by High-Performance Liquid Chromatography-Photodiode Array Detection and Electrospray Ionization-Mass Spectrometry", Chemical & Pharmaceutical Bulletin 56

Li W.-H., Zhang X.-M., Tian R.-R., Zheng Y.-T., Zhao W.-M., Qiu M.-H.,"A new anti-HIV lupane acid from Gleditsia sinensis Lam.". Journal of Asian Natural Products Research. 9. 2007

Lichtenthäler R, Rodrigues RB, Maia JG, Papagiannopoulos M, Fabricius H, Marx F (Feb 2005). "Total oxidant scavenging capacities of Euterpe oleracea Mart. (Açaí) fruits". Int J Food Science Nutrition 56

Lim, T. K. (2013). Edible medicinal and non-medicinal plants. Dordrecht: Springer.

Lin JK, Chen YC, et al. "Suppression of protein kinase C and nuclear oncogene expression as possible molecular mechanism of cancer chemoprevention by apigenin and curcumin", J Cell Biochem

Lin RD, Mao YW, Leu SJ, Huang CY, Lee MH.,"The immuno-regulatory effects of Schisandra chinensis and its constituents on human monocytic leukemia cells." Molecules. 2011

Lis-Balchin M., Hart S. and Simpson E. (2001). Buchu (Agathosma betulina and A. crenulata, Rutaceae) essential oils: their pharmacological action on guinea-pig ileum and antimicrobial activity on microorganisms. J Pharm Pharmacol.

Liu W. Huang XF. Qi Q. Dai QS. Yang L. Nie FF. Lu N. Gong DD. Kong LY. Guo QL. Asparanin A induces G(2)/M cell cycle arrest and apoptosis in human hepatocellular carcinoma HepG2 cells. Biochemical & Biophysical Research Communications. 381

Loewenfeld, C., & Back, P. (1980). Britain's wild larder. North Pomfret, Vt.: David & Charles.

Lohakachornpan P. Chemical compositions and antimicrobial activities of essential oil from Melaleuca leucadendron var. minor. Thai J Pharma Sci. 2001

Longe, J. (2005). The Gale encyclopedia of alternative medicine (2nd ed.). Detroit: Thomson Gale.

Loudon, J. (1866). Loudon's encyclopaedia of plants; comprising the specific character, description, culture, history, application in the arts, and every other desirable particular respecting all the plants indigenous to cultivated in, or introduced into Britain. (New impression. ed.). London: Longmans, Green

Lowther, Granville; William Worthington. The Encyclopedia of Practical Horticulture: A Reference System of Commercial Horticulture, Covering the Practical and Scientific Phases of Horticulture, with Special Reference to Fruits and Vegetables.

Lu, G.; Lu G, Edwards CG, Fellman JK, Mattinson DS, Navazio J. (February 2003). "Biosynthetic origin of geosmin in red beets (Beta vulgaris L.).". Journal of Agricultural and Food Chemistry (abstract) (American Chemical Society) 12

Luczak, S; Swiatek, L; Daniewski, M (1989). "Phenolic acids in herbs Lysimachia nummularia L. And L. Vulgaris L". Acta poloniae pharmaceutica 46

Lynas, L. (1972). Medicinal and food plants of the North American Indians: A bibliography. Bronx, N.Y.: Library of New York Botanical Garden.

M. M. Lolitkar and M. R. Rajarama Rao (1962), Note on a Hypoglycaemic Principle Isolated from the fruits of Momordica charantia. Journal of the University of Bombay, volume 29

Mabey, Richard; 'Plants with a Purpose: A guide to the everyday use of wild plants', William Collins, Fontana, Glasgow, 1977

MacGregor FB, Abernethy VE, Dahabra S, Cobden I, Hayes PC (1989). "Hepatotoxicity of herbal remedies". British Medical Journal 299

Mahadevan, S.; Park, Y. (2007). "Multifaceted Therapeutic Benefits of Ginkgo biloba L.: Chemistry, Efficacy, Safety, and Uses". Journal of Food Science 73

Major Apoptosis-Inducing Components of Bitter Gourd". Journal of Agricultural and Food Chemistry 56

Mandal SC. Kumar C K A. Mohana Lakshmi S. Sinha S. Murugesan T. Saha BP. Pal M. Antitussive effect of Asparagus racemosus root against sulfur dioxide-induced cough in mice. Fitoterapia. 71

Manniche, Lisa; An Ancient Egyptian Herbal, pg. 74; American University in Cairo Press; Cairo; 2006

Marc Spehr; Günter Gisselmann, Alexandra Poplawski, Jeffrey A. Riffell, Christian H. Wetzel, Richard K. Zimmer, Hanns Hatt (2003). "Identification of a Testicular Odorant Receptor Mediating Human Sperm Chemotaxis". Science 299 (5615): 2054.

Marnewick, Jeanine L.; Rautenbach, Fanie; Venter, Irma; Neethling, Henry; Blackhurst, Dee M.; Wolmarans, Petro; Macharia, Muiruri (2011). "Effects of rooibos (Aspalathus linearis) on oxidative stress and biochemical parameters in adults at risk for cardiovascular disease". Journal of Ethnopharmacology 133

Marzouk, B.; Haloui E., Akremi N., Aouni M., Marzouk Z., Fenina N. (2012). "Antimicrobial and anticoagulant activities of Citrullus colocynthis Schrad. leaves from Tunisia (Medenine)". African Journal of Pharmacy and Pharmacology 6

Matlwaska (2002). "Flavonoid compounds in the flowers of Abutilon indicum (Linn.) Sweet". Acia Poloniac Pharmaceutic - Drug Research 59

Matsumoto T., Hosono-Nishiyama K., Yamada H. , "Antiproliferative and apoptotic effects of butyrolactone lignans from Arctium lappa on leukemic cells" Planta Medica 2006

May, G., et al. "Antiviral activity of aqueous extracts from medicinal plants in tissue cultures." Arzneim-Forsch 1978

Mazza, M.; Capuano, A.; Bria, P.; Mazza, S. (2006). "Ginkgo biloba and donepezil: a comparison in the treatment of Alzheimer's dementia in a randomized placebo-controlled double-blind study". European Journal of Neurology 13

McCabe, Melvina; Gohdes, Dorothy; Morgan, Frank; Eakin, Joanne; Sanders, Margaret; Schmitt, Cheryl (2005). "Herbal Therapies and Diabetes Among Navajo Indians". Diabetes Care 28

McCaleb, R., & Leigh, E. (2000). The encyclopedia of popular herbs: Your complete guide to the leading medicinal plants. Roseville, CA: Prima Pub.

McClain, M. (2001). The biogeochemistry of the Amazon Basin. New York: Oxford University Press.

McCutcheon A.R., Stokes W.R., Thorson L.M., Ellis S.M., Hancock R.E.W., Towers G.H.N. Anti-mycobacterial screening of British Columbian medicinal plants. International Journal of Pharmacognosy 1997 35

McDaniel, S.; Goldman, GD (2002). "Consequences of Using Escharotic Agents as Primary Treatment for Nonmelanoma Skin Cancer". Archives of Dermatology 138

McDougall GJ, Ross HA, Ikeji M, Stewart D. 2008. Berry extracts exert different antiproliferative effects against cervical and colon cancer cells grown in vitro. Journal Agricultural Food Chem. 56

McGuffin, M. American Herbal Products Association's botanical safety handbook. American Herbal Products Association.

McKay, Diane L.; Blumberg, Jeffrey B. (2007). "A review of the bioactivity of south African herbal teas: Rooibos (Aspalathus linearis) and honeybush (Cyclopia intermedia)". Phytotherapy Research 21

McKenna, D., & Jones, K. (2011). Botanical Medicines the Desk Reference for Major Herbal Supplements. (Second ed.). New York: Routledge.

Mears, R., & Hillman, G. (2007). Wild food. London: Hodder & Stoughton.

Medeiros RM, de Figueiredo AP, Benício TM, Dantas FP, Riet-Correa F (February 2008). "Teratogenicity of Mimosa tenuiflora seeds to pregnant rats". Toxicon 51

Medicinal Herbs Article list, How to use wild herbs, herb pictures,. (n.d.). Retrieved from http://www.altnature.com/gallery/

MedlinePlus - Health Information from the National Library of Medicine. (n.d.). Retrieved from http://www.nlm.nih.gov/medlineplus/

Mill Goetz P. "Demonstration of the psychotropic effect of mother tincture of Zizyphus jujuba" Phytotherapie 2009

Mills E et al. (2005). "Impact of African herbal medicines on antiretroviral metabolism". AIDS 19

Mills, S. (1985). The dictionary of modern herbalism: A comprehensive guide to practical herbal therapy. New York: Thorsons Pub. Group

Mills, S., & Bone, K. (2000). Principles and practice of phytotherapy: Modern herbal medicine. Edinburgh: Churchill Livingstone.

Miyase T., Yamamoto R., Ueno A.,"Phenylethanoid glycosides from Stachys officinalis" Phytochemistry 1996 43

Moerman, D. (1998). Native American ethnobotany. Portland, Or.: Timber Press.

Mondal, S.; Varma, S.; Bamola, V. D.; Naik, S. N.; Mirdha, B. R.; Padhi, M. M.; Mehta, N.; Mahapatra, S. C. (2011). "Double-blinded randomized controlled trial for immunomodulatory effects of Tulsi (Ocimum sanctum Linn.) leaf extract on healthy volunteers". Journal of Ethnopharmacology 136

Moore, M. (1990). Los Remedios: Traditional Herbal Remedies of the Southwest. Santa Fe, NM: Museum of New Mexico Press.

Mori, S.; Ishikawa, C.; Nakachi, S.; Mori, N. (2011). "Anti-adult T-cell leukemia effects of Bidens pilosa". International Journal of Oncology 38

Mosquito larvicidal activity of oleic and linoleic acids isolated from Citrullus colocynthis (Linn.) Schrad A. Abdul Rahuman, P. Venkatesan and Geetha Gopalakrishnan, Parasitology Research, 2008

Muganza, D., et al. "In vitro antiprotozoal and cytotoxic activity of 33 ethonopharmacologically selected medicinal plants from Democratic Republic of Congo." J Ethnopharmacol. 2012

Mukherjee P.K., Kumar V., Mal M., Houghton P.J. "Acorus calamus: Scientific validation of ayurvedic tradition from natural resources"Pharmaceutical Biology 2007

Muñoz V , Sauvain M , Bourdy G , et al. A search for natural bioactive compounds in Bolivia through a multidisciplinary approach: Part III. Evaluation of the antimalarial activity of plants used by Alteños Indians . J Ethnopharmacol . 2000

NDL/FNIC Food Composition Database. (n.d.). Retrieved from http://ndb.nal.usda.gov/

Naftali T., Feingelernt H., Lesin Y., Rauchwarger A., Konikoff F.M. "Ziziphus jujuba extract for the treatment of chronic idiopathic constipation: A controlled clinical trial" Digestion 2008

Nahrstedt A, Butterweck V (September 1997). "Biologically active and other chemical constituents of the herb of Hypericum perforatum L". Pharmacopsychiatry 30

Nascimento, Gislene G. F.; Locatelli, Juliana; Freitas, Paulo C.; Silva, Giuliana L. (2000). "Antibacterial activity of plant extracts and phytochemicals on antibiotic-resistant bacteria". Brazilian Journal of Microbiology 31

Nathan, P. J.; Tanner, S.; Lloyd, J.; Harrison, B.; Curran, L.; Oliver, C.; Stough, C. (2004). "Effects of a combined extract of Ginkgo biloba and Bacopa monniera on cognitive function in healthy humans". Human Psychopharmacology 19

National Agricultural Library Digital Collections. (n.d.). Retrieved from http://naldc.nal.usda.gov/naldc/home.xhtml

National Center for Complementary and Alternative Medicine

National Library of Medicine - National Institutes of Health. (n.d.). Retrieved from http://www.nlm.nih.gov/

Natural carcinogenic products, EK Weisburger – Environmental Science & Technology, 1979 – ACS Publications

Newton KM, Reed SD, LaCroix AZ, Grothaus LC, Ehrlich K, Guiltinan J (2006). "Treatment of vasomotor symptoms of menopause with black cohosh, multibotanicals, soy, hormone therapy, or placebo: a randomized trial". Annals of Internal Medicine 145

Nielsen, IL; Haren, GR; Magnussen, EL; Dragsted, LO; Rasmussen, SE (2003). "Quantification of anthocyanins in commercial black currant juices by simple high-performance liquid chromatography. Investigation of their pH stability and antioxidative potency". Journal of Agricultural and Food Chemistry 51

Nishanta Rajakaruna, Cory S. Harris and G.H.N. Towers (2002). "Antimicrobial Activity of Plants Collected from Serpentine Outcrops in Sri Lanka". Pharmaceutical Biology 40

Niwano, Y.; et al., Keita; Yoshizaki, Fumihiko; Kohno, Masahiro; Ozawa, Toshihiko (2011). "Extensive screening for herbal extracts with potent antioxidant properties". Journal of Clinical Biochemistry and Nutrition 48

Noosidum A. Excito-repellency properties of essential oils from Melaleuca leucadendron L., Litsea cubeba (Lour.) Persoon and Litsea salicifolia (Nees) on Aedes aegypti (L.) mosquitoes. J Vector Ecol. 2008

Norris, LE; Collene, AL; Asp, ML; Hsu, JC; Liu, LF; Richardson, JR; Li, D, et al. (2009 Sep). "Comparison of dietary conjugated linoleic acid with safflower oil on body composition in obese postmenopausal women with type 2 diabetes mellitus.". The American journal of clinical nutrition 90

Noureddini M., Rasta V.-R. Analgesic Effect of aqueous extract of Achillea millefolium L. on rat's formalin test. Pharmacologyonline 2008

Nuntanakorn P, Jiang B, Yang H, Cervantes-Cervantes M, Kronenberg F, Kennelly EJ (2007). "Analysis of polyphenolic compounds and radical scavenging activity of four American Actaea species". Phytochem Anal 18

Obolskiy D, Pischel I, Siriwatanametanon N, Heinrich M (2009). "Garcinia mangostana L. (mangosteen): A phytochemical and pharmacological review". Phytother Res 23

Ody, P. (2000). Complete guide to medicinal herbs (2nd American ed.). New York: Dorling Kindersley.

Ogihara, Y. (2003). Sho-saiko-to: Scientific evaluation and clinical applications. London: Taylor & Francis.

Ogra, R. K. et al.; Indian calamus (Acorus calamus L.): not a tetraploid; Current Science, Vol. 97, No. 11, 10 December 2009; Current Science Association; Bangalore

Okabe, H.; Miyahara, Y.; Yamauci, T. (1982). "Studies on the constituents of Momordica charantia L.". Chemical Pharmacology Bulletin 30

O'Neill, M. J., et al. "Plants as sources of antimalarial drugs, Part 6. Activities of Simarouba amara fruits." J. Ethnopharmacol. 1988

Online Medical Dictionary. University of Newcastle upon Tyne Centre for Cancer Education. n.d.

Ott, J. (1976). Hallucinogenic Plants of North America. Berkeley, CA: Wingbow Press.

Oyebanji (2011). "Phytochemistry and in vitro anti-oxidant activities of Stellaria media, Cajanus cajan and Tetracera potatoria methanolic extracts". Journal of Medicinal Plants Research 5

Pak K.C., Lam K.Y., Law S., Tang J.C.O.'The inhibitory effect of Gleditsia sinensis on cyclooxygenase-2 expression in human esophageal squamous cell carcinoma." International Journal of Molecular Medicine. 23

Pakistan encyclopaedia planta medica: A joint research project of Hamdard Foundation Pakistan and H.E.J. Research Institute of Chemistry. (1986). Karachi: Hamdard.

Pan, JG; Xu, ZL; Ji, L (1992). "Chemical studies on essential oils from 6 Artemisia species". Zhongguo Zhong yao za zhi 17

Papoutsi Z. Kassi E. Tsiapara A. Fokialakis N. Chrousos GP. Moutsatsou P. (2005). "Evaluation of estrogenic/antiestrogenic activity of ellagic acid via the estrogen receptor subtypes ERalpha and ERbeta". Journal of Agricultural & Food Chemistry 53

Parry, E. (1921). The chemistry of essential oils and artificial perfumes, (4th ed.). London: Scott, Greenwood and Son.

Parry J, Su L, Moore J et al. (May 2006). "Chemical compositions, antioxidant capacities, and antiproliferative activities of selected fruit seed flours". J. Agric. Food Chem. 54

Patel, D. K.; Prasad S.K., Kumar R., Hemalatha S. (2012). "An overview on antidiabetic medicinal plants having insulin mimetic property". Asian Pacific Journal of Tropical Biomedicine 2

Peng, X; Zhao, Y; Liang, X; Wu, L; Cui, S; Guo, A; Wang, W (2006). "Assessing the quality of RCTs on the effect of beta-elemene, one ingredient of a Chinese herb, against malignant tumors". Contemporary clinical trials 27

Perry, Ek; Pickering, At; Wang, Ww; Houghton, P; Perry, Ns (Winter 1998). "Medicinal plants and Alzheimer's disease: Integrating ethnobotanical and contemporary scientific evidence". Journal of alternative and complementary medicine (New York, N.Y.) 4

Phillips, R., & Rix, M. (2002). The botanical garden the definitive reference with more than 2000 photographs. Buffalo, NY: Firefly Books.

Phillips, R., & Rix, M. (2002). The botanical garden: Volume 1 [trees and shrubs]. London: Macmillan. Phillips / Rix

Phillips, R., & Rix, M. (2002). The botanical garden: Volume 2, [perennials and annuals]. London: Macmillan. Phillips / Rix

Physicians' desk reference 2011 (65th ed.). (2010). Montvale, N.J.: Physicians' Desk Reference.

Piacente, S; Carbone, V., Plaza, A., Zampelli, A. & Pizza, C. (2002). "Investigation of the Tuber Constituents of Maca (Lepidium meyenii Walp.)". Journal of Agricultural and Food Chemistry 50

Plant Guide. United States Department of Agriculture Natural Resources Conservation Service. May 30, 2002.

Plants, L. (2000). Proceedings of the National Seminar on the Frontiers of Research and Development in Medicinal Plants: September 16-18, 2000. Lucknow, India: Central Institute of Medicinal and Aromatic Plants.

Platt R (2000). "Current concepts in optimum nutrition for cardiovascular disease". Prev Cardiol 3

Plotkin MJ, Balick MJ (Apr 1984). "Medicinal uses of South American palms". J Ethnopharmacol 10

Polyphenolic Constituents of Fruit Pulp of Euterpe oleracea Mart. (Açai palm). S. Gallori, A. R. Bilia, M. C. Bergonzi, W. L. R. Barbosa and F. F. Vincieri, Chromatographia, 2004

Popovici M., Pârvu A.E., Oniga I., Toiu A., T□maş M., Benedec D. Effects of two Achillea species tinctures on experimental acute inflammation. Farmacia 2008

Potrich F.B., Allemand A., da Silva L.M., dos Santos A.C., Baggio C.H., Freitas C.S., Mendes D.A.G.B., Andre E., de Paula Werner M.F., Marques M.C.A. Antiulcerogenic activity of hydroalcoholic extract of Achillea millefolium L.: Involvement of the antioxidant system. Journal of Ethnopharmacology 2010

Pownall TL, Udenigwe CC, Aluko RE (2010). "Amino acid composition and antioxidant properties of pea seed (Pisum sativum L.) enzymatic protein hydrolysate fractions". Journal of Agricultural and Food Chemistry

Prager N, Bickett K, French N,Marcovici G (2002). "A randomized, double-blind, placebo-controlled trial to determine the effectiveness of botanically derived inhibitors of 5-a-reductase in the treatment of androgenetic alopecia". J Altern Complement Ther 8

Prakash, P.; Gupta, N. (April 2005). "Therapeutic uses of Ocimum sanctum Linn (Tulasi) with a note on eugenol and its pharmacological actions: A short review". Indian Journal of Physiology and Pharmacology 49

Premila, M. (2006). Ayurvedic herbs: A clinical guide to the healing plants of traditional Indian medicine. New York: Haworth Press.

Qiao, C.-Y., Jin-Hua Ran, Yan Li and Xiao-Quan Wang (2007): Phylogeny and Biogeography of Cedrus (Pinaceae) Inferred from Sequences of Seven Paternal Chloroplast and Maternal Mitochondrial DNA Regions. Annals of Botany

Qingdi Q. Li, Gangduo Wang, Manchao Zhang, Christopher F. Cuff, Lan Huang, Eddie Reed (2009). "β-Elemene, a novel plant-derived antineoplastic agent, increases cisplatin chemosensitivity of lung tumor cells by triggering apoptosis". Oncology Reports 22

Qiu SX, Dan C, Ding LS, Peng S, Chen SN, Farnsworth NR, Nolta J, Gross ML, Zhou P (2007). "A triterpene glycoside from black cohosh that inhibits osteoclastogenesis by modulating RANKL and TNFa signaling pathways". Chemistry & Biology 14

Rabbani GH, Butler T, Knight J, Sanyal SC, Alam K (May 1987). "Randomized controlled trial of berberine sulfate therapy for diarrhea due to enterotoxigenic Escherichia coli and Vibrio cholerae". The Journal of Infectious Diseases 155

Rai, V.; Mani, U.V.; Iyer, U.M. (1997). "Effect of Ocimum sanctum Leaf Powder on Blood Lipoproteins, Glycated Proteins and Total Amino Acids in Patients with Non-insulin-dependent Diabetes Mellitus". Journal of Nutritional and Environmental Medicine 7

Randløv C, Mehlsen J, Thomsen CF, Hedman C, von Fircks H, Winther K (March 2006). "The efficacy of St. John's Wort in patients with minor depressive symptoms or dysthymia—a double-blind placebo-controlled study". Phytomedicine 13

Rani, S.; Khan, S.A.; Ali, M. (2010). "Phytochemical investigation of the seeds of Althea officinalis L". Natural Product Research 24

Rastogi, R. (1990). Compendium of Indian medicinal plants. Lucknow: Central Drug Ray RB, Raychoudhuri A, Steele R, Nerurkar P., Bitter Melon (Momordica charantia) Extract Inhibits Breast Cancer Cell Proliferation by Modulating Cell Cycle Regulatory Genes and Promotes Apoptosis. Cancer Res. 2010

Rehder, A. 1940, reprinted 1977. Manual of cultivated trees and shrubs hardy in North America exclusive of the subtropical and warmer temperate regions. Macmillan publishing Co., Inc, New York. Research Institute and Publications & Information Directorate, New Delhi.

Reutera, J.; C. Huykea, H. Scheuvensa, M. Plochc, K. Neumannd, T. Jakobb, C. M. Schemppa (2008). "Skin tolerance of a new bath oil containing St. John's wort extract". Skin pharmacology and physiology 21

Rahman, S., et al. "Anti-tuberculosis activity of quassinoids." Chemical Pharmacology Bulletin. 1997.

Rhoads, Ann F., Timothy A. Block, and Anna Anisko (Illustrator). The Plants of Pennsylvania: An Illustrated Manual, Second edition (2007). University of Pennsylvania Press.

Riddle, John M. (1999). Eve's Herbs: A History of Contraception and Abortion in the West. Harvard University Press.

Riehemann, K; Behnke, B; Schulze-Osthoff, K (1999). "Plant extracts from stinging nettle (Urtica dioica), an antirheumatic remedy, inhibit the proinflammatory transcription factor NF-kappaB". FEBS letters 442

Rinaldi, S. Silva, D. O. Bello, F. Alviano, C S. Alviano, D S. Matheus, ME. Fernandes, P D. (2009). Characterization of the antinociceptive and anti-inflammatory activities from Cocos nucifera L. (Palmae). Journal of Ethnopharmacology 122

Ritchie, F. (1999). Handbook of edible wild plants and weeds. Springfield, Or.: Ritchie Unlimited Publications.

Rivera-Arce E, Chávez-Soto MA, Herrera-Arellano A et al. (February 2007). "Therapeutic effectiveness of a Mimosa tenuiflora cortex extract in venous leg ulceration treatment". J Ethnopharmacol 109

Rivera-Arce E, Gattuso M, Alvarado R et al. (September 2007). "Pharmacognostical studies of the plant drug Mimosae tenuiflorae cortex". J Ethnopharmacol 113

Rodrigues, Eliana & Carlini, E.A. (2006): Plants with possible psychoactive effects used by the Krahô Indians, Brazil. Revista Brasileira de Psiquiatria

Roodenrys, S.; Booth, D.; Bulzomi, S.; Phipps, A.; Micallef, C.; Smoker, J. (2002). "Chronic effects of Brahmi (Bacopa monnieri) on human memory". Neuropsychopharmacology 27

Rose, J. (1987). Jeanne Rose's modern herbal. New York, N.Y.: Perigee Books.

Rosengarten, Frederic, Jr. (2004). The Book of Edible Nuts. Dover Publications.

Ross, I. (1999). Medicinal plants of the world: Chemical constituents, traditional, and modern medicinal uses. Totowa, N.J.: Humana Press.

Ross, J. (2003). Combining Western herbs and Chinese medicine: Principles, practice, and materia medica. Seattle, Wash.: Greenfields Press.

Roy, K.; Thakur M., Dixit V.K. (2007). "Effect of Citrullus colocynthis on hair growth in albino rats". Pharmaceutical Biology 45

Royal Horticultural Society; http://apps.rhs.org.uk/plantselector/

Said, O., Khalil, K. Fulder, S. and Azaizeh, H. Ethnopharmacological Survey of the Medicinal herbs in Israel, the Golan Heights and the West Bank Region. Journal of Ethnopharmacology, 83

Sairam K. Priyambada S. Aryya NC. Goel RK.Gastroduodenal ulcer protective activity of Asparagus racemosus: an experimental, biochemical and histological study. Journal of Ethnopharmacology. 86

Sale C, Harris RC, Delves S, Corbett J (May 2006). "Metabolic and physiological effects of ingesting extracts of bitter orange, green tea and guarana at rest and during treadmill walking in overweight males". Int J Obes (Lond) 30

Salunkhe, D.K., J.K. Chavan, R.N. Adsule, and S.S. Kadam. (1992). World Oilseeds – Chemistry, Technology, and Utilization. Springer.

Samorini, Giorgio (2002). Animals and psychedelics: the natural world and the instinct to alter consciousness.

Sayyah, M.; Saroukhani, G.; Peirovi, A.; Kamalinejad, M. (August 2003).

"Analgesic and anti-inflammatory activity of the leaf essential oil of Laurus nobilis Linn". Phytother Res 17

Schafferman, D.; Beharav A., Shabelsky E., Yaniv Z (1998). "Evaluation of Citrullus colocynthis, a desert plant native in Israel, as a potential source of edible oil". Journal of Arid Environments 40

Schauss A.G., Wu X., Prior R.L., Ou B., Huang D., Owens J., Agarwal A., Jensen G.S., Hart A.N., Shanbrom E. (2006). "Antioxidant capacity and other bioactivities of the freeze-dried amazonian palm berry, Euterpe oleraceae Mart. (acai)". J Agric Food Chem 54

Schnitzler, P; Schuhmacher, A; Astani, A; Reichling, J (2008). "Melissa officinalis oil affects infectivity of enveloped herpesviruses". Phytomedicine 15

Scholey, A B (2003). "Modulation of Mood and Cognitive Performance Following Acute Administration of Single Doses of Melissa Officinalis (Lemon Balm) with Human CNS Nicotinic and Muscarinic Receptor-Binding Properties". Neuropsychopharmacology 28

Schubert SY, Lansky EP, Neeman I (July, 1999). "Antioxidant and eicosanoid enzyme inhibition properties of pomegranate seed oil and fermented juice flavonoids". J Ethnopharmacol 66

Schultz, Gretchen; Peterson, Chris; Coats, Joel (2006). "Natural Insect Repellents: Activity against Mosquitoes and Cockroaches"

Schulz, V. (2004). Rational phytotherapy: A reference guide for physicians and pharmacists (5th ed.). Berlin: Springer.

Seal S, Chatterjee P, Bhattacharya S, Pal D, Dasgupta S, et al. (2012) Vapor of Volatile Oils from Litsea cubeba Seed Induces Apoptosis and Causes Cell Cycle Arrest in Lung Cancer Cells. PLoS ONE 7

Seden K. Dickinson L. Khoo S. Back D.. Grapefruit-drug interactions. [Review]. Drugs. 2010. 70.

Sheeja K, Shihab PK, Kuttan G. Antioxidant and inflammatory modulating activities of the plant Andrographis paniculata Nees, Immunopharmacol Immunotoxicol. 2006.

Seeram NP, Aronson WJ, Zhang Y et al. (September 2007). "Pomegranate ellagitannin-derived metabolites inhibit prostate cancer growth and localize to the mouse prostate gland". J. Agric. Food Chem. 55

Semiz, A, Sen A. (February 2007). "Antioxidant and chemoprotective properties of Momordica charantia L. (bitter melon) fruit extract". African Journal of Biotechnology 6

Seeram, NP (2008). "Berry fruits: compositional elements, biochemical activities, and the impact of their intake on human health, performance, and disease". Journal of Agricultural and Food Chemistry 56

Seidl, P. (1995). Chemistry of the Amazon: Biodiversity, natural products, and environmental issues : Developed from the First International Symosium on Chemistry and the Amazon sponsored by the Associação Brasileira de Química, American Chemical Semiz, A, Sen A. (February 2007). "Antioxidant and chemoprotective properties of Momordica charantia L. (bitter melon) fruit extract". African Journal of Biotechnology 6

Seo SW et al. (Jan 2011). "Protective effects of Curcuma longa against cerulein-induced acute pancreatitis and pancreatitis-associated lung injury". Int J Mol Med 27

Sharma K. Bhatnagar M. Kulkarni SK. "Effect of Convolvulus pluricaulis Choisy and Asparagus racemosus Willd on learning and memory in young and old mice: a comparative evaluation." Indian Journal of Experimental Biology. 48

Sharma, P.; Kulshreshtha, S.; Sharma, A.L. (1998). "Anti-cataract activity of Ocimum sanctum on experimental cataract". Indian Journal of Pharmacology 30

Sharma U. Saini R. Kumar N. Singh B. Steroidal saponins from Asparagus racemosus. Chemical & Pharmaceutical Bulletin. 57

Shi J, Yu J, Pohorly JE, Kakuda Y (2003). "Polyphenolics in grape seeds-biochemistry and functionality". Journal Medicinal Food 6

Shibib, BA; Khan, LA; Rahman, R (May 15). "Hypoglycemic activity of Coccinia indica and Momordica charantia in diabetic rats: depression of the hepatic gluconeogenic enzymes glucose-6-phosphatase and fructose-1,6-bisphosphatase and elevation of both liver and red-cell shunt enzyme glucose-6-phosphate dehydrogenase". Biochem J. 292

Shin HR, Kim JY, Yun TK, Morgan G, Vainio H (2000). 'The cancer-preventive potential of Panax ginseng: a review of human and experimental evidence". Cancer Causes Control 11

Shukla, A.; Rasik, A. M.; Jain, G. K.; Shankar, R.; Kulshrestha, D. K.; Dhawan, B. N. (1999). "In vitro and in vivo wound healing activity of asiaticoside isolated from Centella asiatica". Journal of Ethnopharmacology 65

Shukla PK, Khanna VK, Ali MM, Maurya R, Khan MY, Srimal RC. "Neuroprotective effect of Acorus calamus against middle cerebral artery occlusion-induced ischaemia in rat" Hum Exp Toxicology 2006.

Silva FL, Fischer DC, Tavares JF, Silva MS, de Athayde-Filho PF, Barbosa-Filho JM.,"Compilation of secondary metabolites from Bidens pilosa L." Molecules, 2011

Simic, M; Kundaković, T; Kovacević, N (September 2003). "Preliminary assay on the antioxidative activity of Laurus nobilis extracts". Fitoterapia 74

Simon PW (1997). Plant Pigments for Color and Nutrition.

Singh, A.; Singh, S. K. (2009). "Evaluation of antifertility potential of Brahmi in male mouse". Contraception 79

Singh GK. Garabadu D. Muruganandam AV. Joshi VK. Krishnamurthy S. Antidepressant activity of Asparagus racemosus in rodent models. Pharmacology, Biochemistry & Behavior. 91

Sinisalo, Marjatta; Enkovaara, Anna-Liisa; Kivistö, Kari T. (2010). "Possible hepatotoxic effect of rooibos tea: A case report". European Journal of Clinical Pharmacology 66

Small, E., & Catling, P. (1999). Canadian medicinal crops. Ottawa: NRC Research Press.

Society, Centro de Tecnologia Mineral, and Instituto Nacional de Pesquisas da Amazonia Manaus, Amazonas, Brazil, November 21-25, 1993. Washington, DC:

Smith, A, (1997). A Gardener's Handbook of Plant Names: Their Meanings and Origins. Dover Publications

Smith, P; MacLennan, K; Darlington, CL (1996). "The neuroprotective

157

properties of the Ginkgo biloba leaf: a review of the possible relationship to platelet-activating factor (PAF)". Journal of Ethnopharmacology 50

Stuart, M. (1981). The Encyclopedia of herbs and herbalism. New York: Crescent Books

South, G., & Whittick, A. (1987). Introduction to phycology. Oxford [Oxfordshire: Blackwell Scientific Publications.

Stablein JJ. Melaleuca tree and respiratory disease. Ann Allergy Asthma Immunol. 2002

Standley, L; Winterton, P; Marnewick, JL; Gelderblom, WC; Joubert, E; Britz, TJ (2001 Jan). "Influence of processing stages on antimutagenic and antioxidant potentials of rooibos tea.". Journal of Agricultural and Food Chemistry 49

Stough, C.; Downey, L. A.; Lloyd, J.; Silber, B.; Redman, S.; Hutchison, C.; Wesnes, K.; Nathan, P. J. (2008). "Examining the nootropic effects of a special extract of Bacopa Monniera on human cognitive functioning: 90 day double-blind placebo-controlled randomized trial". Phytotherapy Research 22

Streloke, M. et al.; Ascher, K. R. S.; Schmidt, G. H.; Neumann, W. P. (1989). "Vapor pressure and volatility of β-asarone, the main ingredient of an indigenous stored-product insecticide, Acorus calamus oil". Phytoparasitica 17

Sturtevant, WC (1955). The Mikasuki Seminole: Medical Beliefs and Practices. Ann Arbor, MI: University Microfilms.

Stuttgart: Georg Thieme Verlag. Biology and chemistry of active natural substances: International symposium, Bonn, July 17-22, 1990, plenary lectures. (1991).

Suanarunsawat, T.; Boonnak, T.; Na Ayutthaya, W. D.; Thirawarapan, S. (2010). "Anti-hyperlipidemic and cardioprotective effects of Ocimum sanctum L. fixed oil in rats fed a high fat diet". Journal of Basic and Clinical Physiology and Pharmacology 21

Suh SO, Kroh M, Kim NR, Joh YG, Cho MY. (2002). "Effects of red ginseng upon postoperative immunity and survival in patients with stage III gastric cancer". American Journal of Chinese Medicine. 30

Sultan S, Spector J, Mitchell RM (December 2006). "Ischemic colitis associated with use of a bitter orange-containing dietary weight-loss supplement". Mayo Clinic Proceedings 81

Sun, Meng; Lou, Wei; Chun, Jae Yeon; Cho, Daniel S.; Nadiminty, Nagalakshmi; Evans, Christopher P. et al. (2010). "Sanguinarine Suppresses Prostate Tumor Growth and Inhibits Survivin Expression". Genes & Cancer 1

Szapary, PO; Wolfe, ML; Bloedon, LT; Cucchiara, AJ; Dermarderosian, AH; Cirigliano, MD; Rader, DJ (2003). "Guggulipid Ineffective for Lowering Cholesterol". JAMA 290

T. Ogasawara, k.Chiba, m.Tada in (Y. P. S. Bajaj ed). 1988. Medicinal and Aromatic Plants, Volume 10. Springer,

Taati, Majid; Masoud Alirezaei, Mohamad Hadi Moshkatalsadat, Bahram Rasoulian, Mehrnoush Moghadasi, Farzam Sheikhzadeh, Ali Sokhtezari. (2011). "Protective effects of Ziziphus jujuba fruit extract against ethanol-induced hippocampal oxidative stress and spatial memory impairment in rats". Journal of Medicinal Plants Research 5

Tan, NH; Fung, SY; Sim, SM; Marinello, E; Guerranti, R; Aguiyi, JC (2009). "The protective effect of Mucuna pruriens seeds against snake venom poisoning". Journal of Ethnopharmacology 123

Tanacetum Balsamita L: A Medicinal Plant. M.J. Pérez-Alonso, A. Velasco-Negueruela, A. Burzaco

Tang J., Wang C.K., Pan X., Yan H., Zeng G., Xu W., He W., Daly N.L., Craik D.J., Tan N."Isolation and characterization of cytotoxic cyclotides from Viola tricolor" Peptides 2010

Tang SY, Gruber J, Wong KP, Halliwell B (April 2007). "Psoralea corylifolia L. inhibits mitochondrial complex I and proteasome activities in SH-SY5Y cells". Ann. N. Y. Acad. Sci. 1100: 486–96.

Tang W.K., Chui C.H., Fatima S., Kok S.H., Pak K.C., Ou T.M., Hui K.S., Wong M.M., Wong J., Law S., Tsao S.W., Lam K.Y., Beh P.S., Srivastava G., Ho K.P., Chan A.S., Tang J.C. "Inhibitory effects of Gleditsia sinensis fruit extract on telomerase activity and oncogenic expression in human esophageal squamous cell carcinoma." International journal of molecular medicine. 19. 2007.

Tannin-Spitz, T.; Grossman S., Dovrat S., Gottlieb H.E., Bergman M. (2007). "Growth inhibitory activity of cucurbitacin glucosides isolated from Citrullus colocynthis on human breast cancer cells". Biochemical Pharmacology 73

Tatsis, EC; Boeren, S; Exarchou, V; Troganis, AN; Vervoort, J; Gerothanassis, IP (2007). "Identification of the major constituents of Hypericum perforatum by LC/SPE/NMR and/or LC/MS". Phytochemistry 68

Taur D.J., Patil R.Y.,"Mast cell stabilizing, antianaphylactic and antihistaminic activity of Coccinia grandis fruits in asthma". Chinese Journal of Natural Medicines. 9

Taylor, Frederick R. (2011). "Nutraceuticals and Headache: The Biological Basis". Headache: the Journal of Head and Face Pain 51

Taylor LG (2005). The healing power of rainforest herbs: a guide to understanding and using herbal medicinals. Garden City Park, NY: Square One Publishers.

Teschke, R; Bahre, R (2009). "Severe hepatotoxicity by Indian Ayurvedic herbal products: A structured causality assessment". Annals of hepatology 8.

Teucher, T; Obertreis, B; Ruttkowski, T; Schmitz, H (1996). "Cytokine secretion in whole blood of healthy subjects following oral administration of Urtica dioica L. Plant extract". Arzneimittel-Forschung 46

Thakur M. Chauhan NS. Bhargava S. Dixit VK. A comparative study on aphrodisiac activity of some ayurvedic herbs in male albino rats. Archives of Sexual Behavior. 38

The Organic Gardener's Handbook of Natural Pest and Disease, Fern Marshall Bradley, Barbara W. Ellis, Deborah L. Martin,

The pharmacopœia of the United States of America: (the United States pharmacopœia). (12th revision (U.S.P. XII) / ed.). (1942). Washington, D.C.: Published by the Board of Trustees

The Pharmacopoeia of the United States of America (The United States pharmacopoeia) 19th rev. (1974). Rockville, Md.: United States Pharmacopeial Convention.

The use of herbal medicines by people with cancer: A qualitative study. (2009). BioMed Central.

"Therapeutic effect of arctiin and arctigenin in immunocompetent and immunocompromised mice infected with influenza" Biological and Pharmaceutical Bulletin 2010

Thierer, John W., Niering, William A., and Olmstead, Nancy C. (2001) National Audubon Society Field Guide to North American Wildflowers, Eastern Region, Revised Edition. Alfred A. Knopf

Thompson LU, Chen JM, Li T, Strasser-Weippl K, Goss PE (2005). "Dietary flaxseed alters tumor biological markers in postmenopausal breast cancer". Clinical Cancer Research 11

Thomson, W. (1978). Healing Plants: A modern herbal. London: Macmillan.

Tipton, K. (1979). Neurochemistry and biochemical pharmacology. Baltimore: University Park Press.

Tiwari M, Dwivedi UN, Kakkar P. 2010. Suppression of oxidative stress and pro-inflammatory mediators by Cymbopogon citratus D. Stapf extract in lipopolysaccharide stimulated murine alveolar macrophages. Food Chemistry Toxicology

Toiu A. Muntean E. Oniga I. Vostinaru O. Tamas M. " Pharmacognostic research on Viola tricolor L. (Violaceae)." Revista Medico-Chirurgicala a Societatii de Medici Si Naturalisti Din Iasi. 1

Toiu A. Parvu AE. Oniga I. Tamas M."Evaluation of anti-inflammatory activity of alcoholic extract from Viola tricolor.", Revista Medico-Chirurgicala a Societatii de Medici Si Naturalisti Din Iasi. 11

Trease, G. (1952). A Text-Book of Pharmacognosy ... Sixth edition. Pp. viii. 821. Baillière, Tindall & Cox: London.

Tsch, C. (2005). The encyclopedia of psychoactive plants: Ethnopharmacology and its applications. Rochester, Vt.: Park Street Press.

Tsuda H; Ohshima Y; Nomoto H et al. (2004). "Cancer prevention by natural compounds". Drug Metabolism and Pharmacokinetics 19

Tulyaganov, T. S.; Nigmatullaev, A. M. (2000). Chemistry of Natural Compounds 36

Tutin, T. (1976). Flora Europaea. Cambridge: Cambridge University Press.

Ukiya M, Akihisa T, Yasukawa K et al. Anti-inflammatory, anti-tumor-promoting, and cytotoxic activities of constituents of pot marigold (Calendula officinalis) flowers. (2006).

Umek, A; Kreft, S; Kartnig, T; Heydel, B (1999). "Quantitative phytochemical analyses of six hypericum species growing in slovenia". Planta medica 65

UN Food & Agriculture Organisation | Online references | cyclopaedia.net. (n.d.). Retrieved from http://www.cyclopaedia.info/UN-Food-and-Agriculture-Organisation

Valdes, A., et al. "In vitro anti-microbial activity of the Cuban medicinal plants Simarouba glauca DC, Melaleuca leucadendron L and Artemisia absinthium L." Mem Inst Oswaldo Cruz. 2008

Valeriote, F. A., et al. "Anticancer activity of glaucarubinone analogues." Oncol Res. 1998

Vaughan, J.G.; Geissler, C.A. (1997). The New Oxford Book of Food Plants. Oxford University Press.

Veronese ML, Gillen LP, Burke JP, Dorval EP, Hauck WW, Pequignot E, Waldman SA, Greenberg HE. Exposure-dependent inhibition of intestinal and hepatic CYP3A4 in vivo by grapefruit juice. Journal of Clinical Pharmacology. 2003;43

Visarata, N.; Ungsurungsie, M. (1981). "Extracts from Momordica charantiaL". Pharmaceutical Biology 19

Volz, S. M., and S. S. Renner (Volz and Renner) 2009. Phylogeography of the ancient Eurasian medicinal plant genus Bryonia (Cucurbitaceae) inferred from nuclear and chloroplast sequences. Taxon 58

von Woedtke T, Schlüter B, Pflegel P, Lindequist U, Jülich WD (June 1999). "Aspects of the antimicrobial efficacy of grapefruit seed extract and its relation to preservative substances contained". Pharmazie 54

Vukics V. Kery A. Guttman A."Analysis of polar antioxidants in Heartsease (Viola tricolor L.) and Garden pansy (Viola x wittrockiana Gams.)". Journal of Chromatographic Science. 46

Waako PJ, Gumede B, Smith P, Folb PI (May 2005). "The in vitro and in vivo antimalarial activity of Cardiospermum halicacabum L. and Momordica foetida Schumch. Et Thonn". J Ethnopharmacol 99

Wada L, Ou B (June 2002). "Antioxidant activity and phenolic content of Oregon caneberries". Journal of Agricultural and Food Chemistry 50

Wagh S., Vidhale N.N. (2010). "Antimicrobial efficacy of Boerhaavia diffusa against some human pathogenic bacteria and fungi". Biosciences Biotechnology Research Asia 7

Wagner, Hildebert (1999). Immunomodulatory agents from plants. Birkhäuser.

Wang C., Xia Y.F., Gao Z.Z., Lu D., Dai Y. "Inhibition of mast cell degranulation by saponins from Gleditsia sinensis- structure-activity relationships." Natural Product Communications. 4. 2009

Wang JJ, Shi QH, Zhang W, Sanderson BJ (2012). "Anti-skin cancer properties of phenolic-rich extract from the pericarp of mangosteen (Garcinia mangostana Linn.)". Food Chemistry Toxicology 50

Wang, Lu et al. (2009). "Ultrasonic nebulization extraction coupled with headspace single drop microextraction and gas chromatography–mass spectrometry for analysis of the essential oil in Cuminum cyminum L". Analytica Chimica Acta 647

Wang ZT, Ng TB, Yeung HW, Xu GJ (December 1996). "Immunomodulatory effect of a polysaccharide-enriched preparation of Codonopsis pilosula roots". Gen. Pharmacol. 27 Warrier, P. K.; V. P. K. Nambiar, C. Ramankutty, R. Vasudevan Nair (1996). Indian medicinal plants. Orient Blackswan.

Weber HA, Zart MK, Hodges AE, et al. (December 2003). "Chemical comparison of goldenseal (Hydrastis canadensis L.) root powder from three commercial suppliers". Journal of Agricultural and Food Chemistry 51

Weber W, Vander Stoep A, McCarty RL, Weiss NS, Biederman J, McClellan J (June 2008). "A Randomized Placebo Controlled Trial Of Hypericum perforatum For Attention Deficit Hyperactivity Disorder In Children And Adolescents". JAMA 299

Webster, D.E.; J. Lu, S.-N. Chen, N.R. Farnsworth and Z. Jim Wang (2006). "Activation of the μ-opiate receptor by Vitex agnus-castus methanol extracts: Implication for its use in PMS". Journal of Ethnopharmacology 106

Weerasinghe, Priya; Hallock, Sarathi; Brown, Robert E.; Loose, David S.; Buja, L. Maximilian (2012). "A model for cardiomyocyte cell death: Insights into mechanisms of oncosis". Experimental and Molecular Pathology.

Weinmann, S; Roll, S; Schwarzbach, C; Vauth, C; Willich, SN (2010). "Effects of Ginkgo biloba in dementia: systematic review and meta-analysis". BMC geriatrics 10

Weisskopf. Schaffner. Jundt. Sulser. Wyler. Tullberg-Reinert. Planta Medica 2005

Wells, A., Edwards, E.D., Houston, W. W. K., Lepidoptera: Hesperioidea, Papilionoidea, Volume 31, CSIRO, 2001.

Wheatley D (2004). "Triple-blind, placebo-controlled trial of Ginkgo biloba in sexual dysfunction due to antidepressant drugs". Hum Psychopharmacol 19.

Wilt TJ, Ishani A, Rutks I, MacDonald R (2000). "Phytotherapy for benign prostatic hyperplasia". Public Health Nutr 3

Winston, David & Maimes, Steven. "Adaptogens: Herbs for Strength, Stamina, and Stress Relief," Healing Arts Press, 2007.

Whitford AC (1941). "Textile fibers used in eastern aboriginal North America". Anthropological Papers of the American Museum of Natural History 38

Wichtl, Max,Herbal drugs and phytopharmaceuticals: a handbook,2004

Wild Medicinal Plants: What to Look For, When to Harvest, How to Use 2002 Schneider / Mellichamp

William Thomas Fernie, Herbal Simples Approved for Modern Uses of Cure, 3rd enlarged ed. Bristol: Wright, 1914

Williamson, E. (2009). Stockley's herbal medicines interactions a guide to the interactions of herbal medicines, dietary supplements and nutraceuticals with conventional medicines. London: Pharmaceutical Press.

Wilt T, Ishani A, Mac Donald R (2002). "Serenoa repens for benign prostatic hyperplasia". In Tacklind, James. Cochrane Database Syst Rev (3): CD001423.

Winston & Kuhn's Herbal Therapy & Supplements: A Scientific and Traditional Approach 2007 Kuhn / Winston

Witkowska-Banaszczak E., Bylka W., Matławska I., Goślińska O., Muszyński Z. ,"Antimicrobial activity of Viola tricolor herb". Fitoterapia 2005

Wong AHC, Smith M, Boon HS (1998). "Herbal remedies in psychiatric practice". Arch Gen Psychiatry 55

Wright CI, Van-Buren L, Kroner CI, Koning MM (October 2007). "Herbal medicines as diuretics: a review of the scientific evidence". J Ethnopharmacol 114

Wright SC. Maree JE. Sibanyoni M. Treatment of oral thrush in HIV/AIDS patients with lemon juice and lemon grass (Cymbopogon citratus) and gentian violet. Phytomedicine. 16. 2009.

Wyk, B., & Wink, M. (2004). Medicinal plants of the world: An illustrated scientific guide to important medicinal plants and their uses. Portland: Timber Press.

Xie L.-H., Ahn E.-M., Akao T., Abdel-Hafez A.A.-M., Nakamura N., Hattori M."Transformation of arctiin to estrogenic and antiestrogenic substances by human intestinal bacteria" Chemical and Pharmaceutical Bulletin 2003

Xu XM, Li L, Chen M., "Studies on the chemical constituents of Schisandra pubescens". Zhong Yao Cai. 2009

Xu Y.J., Han C.J., Xu S.J., Yu X., Jiang G.Z., Nan C.H. "Effects of Acanthopanax senticosus on learning and memory in a mouse model of

Alzheimer's disease and protection against free radical injury to brain tissue" Neural Regeneration Research 2008

Yamada, K.; Hung, P.; Park, T. K.; Park, P. J.; Limb, B. O. (2011). "A comparison of the immunostimulatory effects of the medicinal herbs Echinacea, Ashwagandha and Brahmi". Journal of Ethnopharmacology 137

Yemm RS, Poulton JE (June 1986). "Isolation and characterization of multiple forms of mandelonitrile lyase from mature black cherry (Prunus serotina Ehrh.) seeds". Archives of biochemistry and biophysics 247

Yeung, H. (1985). Handbook of Chinese herbs and formulas. Los Angeles, U.S.A.: H.C. Yeung.

Yeung. Him-Che. Handbook of Chinese Herbs and Formulas. 1985. Los Angeles: Institute of Chinese Medicine.

Yoo, Ki-Yeon; Hua Li, In Koo Hwang, Jung Hoon Choi, Choong Hyun Lee, Dae Young Kwon, Shi Yong Ryu, Young Sup Kim, Il-Jun Kang, Hyung-Cheul Shin, and Moo-Ho Won. (2010). "Zizyphus Attenuates Ischemic Damage in the Gerbil Hippocampus via Its Antioxidant Effect". Journal of Medicinal Food 13

Yoshikawa M, Murakami T, Kishi A et al. (2001). Medicinal flowers. III. Marigold.(1): hypoglycemic, gastric emptying inhibitory, and gastroprotective principles and new oleanane-type triterpene oligolycosides, calendasaponins A, B, C, and D, from Egyptian Calendula officinalis. Chem Pharm

Yu, Xiuzhu; Van De Voort, Frederick R.; Li, Zhixi; Yue, Tianli (2007). "Proximate Composition of the Apple Seed and Characterization of Its Oil".

International Journal of Food Engineering 3

Yuan CS, Mehendale S, Xiao Y, Aung HH, Xie JT, Ang-Lee MK (2004). "The gamma-aminobutyric acidergic effects of valerian and valerenic acid on rat brainstem neuronal activity.". Anesth Analg 98

Yun TK, Lee YS, Lee YH, Kim SI, Yun HY (2001). "Anticarcinogenic effect of Panax ginseng C.A. Meyer and identification of active compounds". Journal of Korean Medical Science 16

Zakay-Rones, Zichria; Noemi Varsano, Moshe Zlotnik, Orly Manor, Liora Regev, Miriam Schlesinger, Madeleine Mumcuoglu (1995). "Inhibition of Several Strains of Influenza Virus in Vitro and Reduction of Symptoms by an Elderberry Extract (Sambucus nigra L.) during an Outbreak of Influenza B Panama" (PDF). J Altern Complement Med 1

Zakim, D. (1985). Biochemical pharmacology and toxicology. New York: Wiley. Biochemical Pharmacology. 2011

Zarse, K., et al. "The phytochemical glaucarubinone promotes mitochondrial metabolism, reduces body fat, and extends lifespan of Caenorhabditis elegans." Horm Metab Res. 2011

Zhang XW, Li WF, Li WW, Ren KH, Fan CM, Chen YY, Shen YL (2011). "Protective effects of the aqueous extract of Scutellaria baicalensis against acrolein-induced oxidative stress in cultured human umbilical vein endothelial cells". Pharm Biol 49

Zhao F., Wang L., Liu K. "In vitro anti-inflammatory effects of arctigenin, a lignan from Arctium lappa L., through inhibition on iNOS pathway" Journal of Ethnopharmacology 2009

Zhao G, Li S, Qin GW, Fei J, Guo LH (2007). "Inhibitive effects of Fructus Psoraleae extract on dopamine transporter and noradrenaline transporter.". J Ethnopharmacol 112 (3): 498–506.

Zhou L., Li D., Wang J., Liu Y., Wu J."Antibacterial phenolic compounds from the spines of Gleditsia sinensis Lam." Natural Product Research. 21. 2007.

Zhao LH, Huang CY, Shan Z, Xiang BG, Mei LH (2005). "Fingerprint analysis of Psoralea corylifolia by HLPC and LC-MS". J Chromatogr B 821: 67–74.

Zhu X. Zhang W. Zhao J. Wang J. Qu W. Hypolipidaemic and hepatoprotective effects of ethanolic and aqueous extracts from Asparagus officinalis L. by-products in mice fed a high-fat diet. Journal of the Science of Food & Agriculture. 90

Zick S.M., Sen A., Feng Y., Green J., Olatunde S., Boon H."Trial of essiac to ascertain its effect in women with breast cancer (TEA-BC)" Journal of Alternative and Complementary Medicine 2006

Zillur Rahman and M. Shamim Jairajpuri. Neem in Unani Medicine. Neem Research and Development Society of Pesticide Science, India, New Delhi, 1993. Edited by N.S. Randhawa and B.S. Parmar. 2nd revised edition

Spencer, C. F., et al. "Survey of plants for antimalarial activity." Lloydia 1947

www.ingramcontent.com/pod-product-compliance
Lightning Source LLC
Chambersburg PA
CBHW082356270326
41935CB00013B/1645